The Official Story of Arsenal's Double Year

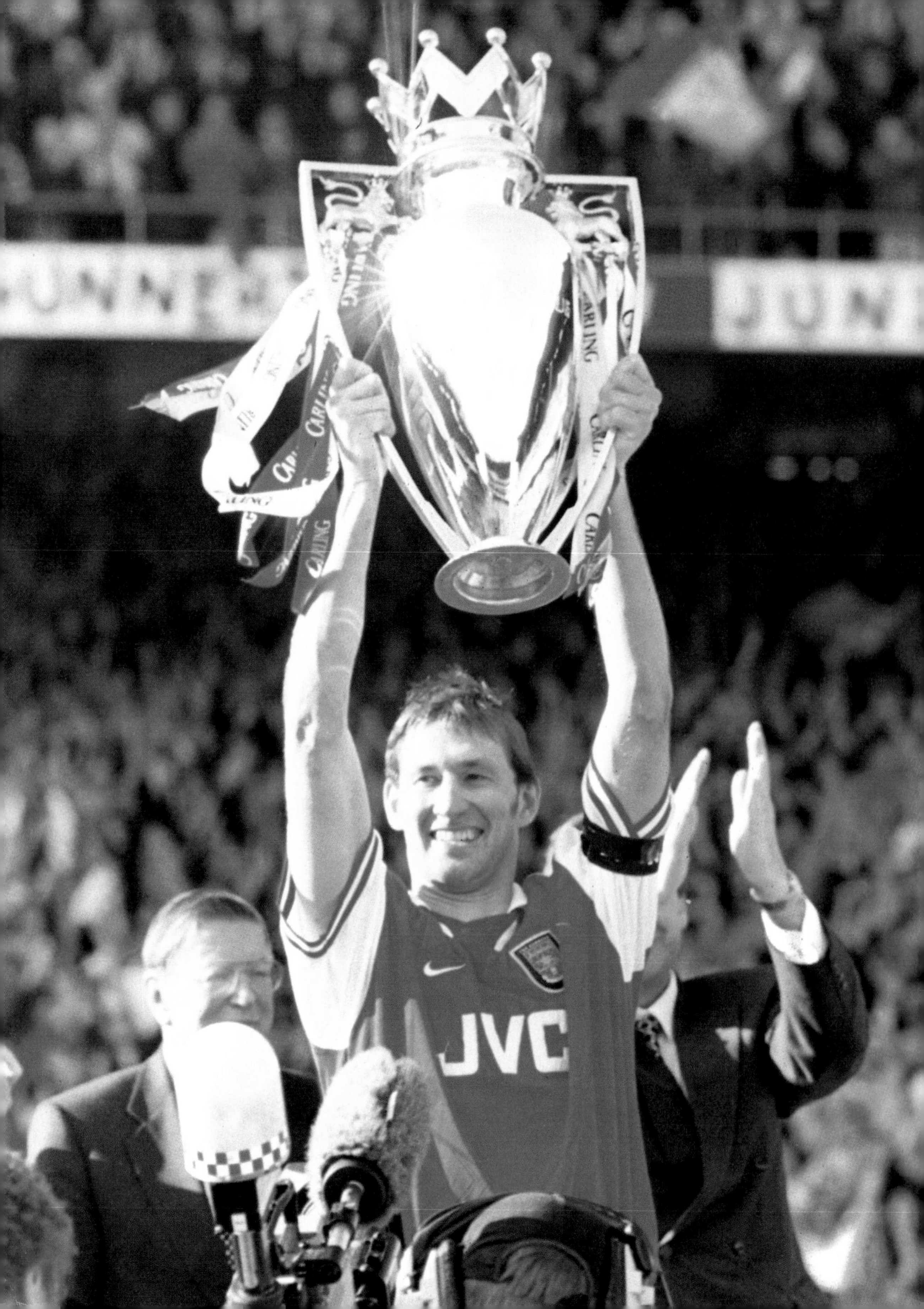
CARLING
JVC

The Official Story of Arsenal's Double Year

KEVIN CONNOLLY

Introduction by Tony Adams

HEADLINE

First published in 1998 by
HEADLINE BOOK PUBLISHING
10 9 8 7 6 5 4 3 2 1

ISBN 0 7472 7544 0

Typeset and designed by Isobel Gillan
Printed and bound in Great Britain by
Bath Press Colour Books

HEADLINE BOOK PUBLISHING
A division of Hodder Headline PLC
338 Euston Road
London NW1 3BH

Previous page Tony Adams lifts the Championship trophy.

CONTENTS

INTRODUCTION
by Tony Adams

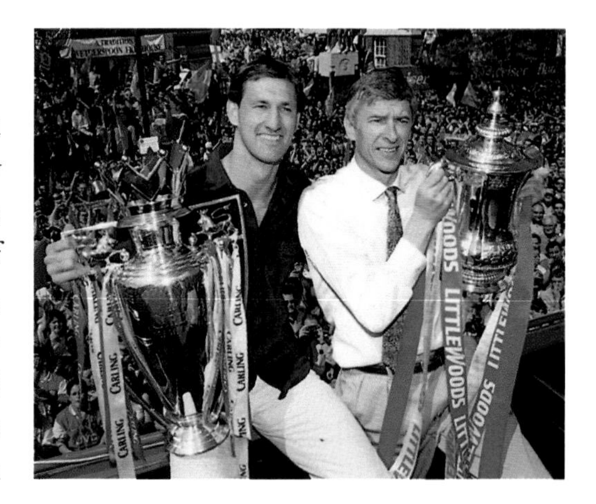

Tony Adams and Arsène Wenger display the Gunners' Double trophies on the parade to Islington town hall.

What a season that was! They were two of the proudest moments of my footballing life, lifting the Championship trophy on 3 May, and then the FA Cup thirteen days later. What made the achievement even more satisfying was how we did it: coming from way behind in the title race, then taking the FA Cup by winning six ties away from Highbury.

It's always been an Arsenal trait, to overcome difficulties and prove our critics wrong. At Christmas and even early in the New Year, we were being written off. But there was tremendous determination in the dressing room. Arsène Wenger kept calm and the players all supported each other. When I came back from my rehab spell in France, I could sense the mood in the camp.

The season began with high hopes after M. Wenger's summer signings. I'd never heard so many different accents in the dressing room! I think players of ability who are prepared to work for the team soon gain respect, whatever the language. That was certainly the case with our new signings. What takes time, though, is adapting to the particular demands of English football, as Dennis Bergkamp and Patrick Vieira will both confirm.

Once our new players had done that, they made vital contributions to our success. Marc Overmars gave us so many more options in attack. He usually attracted two defenders' attention, which freed more space for other players. Manu Petit was magnificent on the Championship run-in, and it was great to see him getting among the goalscorers. Gilles Grimandi proved himself a valuable defender, covering at right-back or in the centre – and his goal against Crystal Palace was priceless. Luis Boa Morte has bags of pace. Alberto Mendez was unlucky with injuries after impressing in the reserves. Chris Wreh came on very quickly after Christmas, once he'd learned what was required. He scored some hugely important goals – though I don't think I'd ever try one of his somersault celebrations!

If anyone showed how fast he'd adapted to the English game, though, it was Nicolas Anelka. Within five months, he developed from an inexperienced striker into someone who carried a big threat. He has terrific pace and control. He built up his strength to cope with the physical side of the game. Having a long run in the side also built up his confidence, because he learned something from every match.

The way Nicolas and Chris stepped in, when Dennis and Wrighty were out, was very important. Alex Manninger was also a terrific deputy for David Seaman. He looks a goalkeeper of huge potential. He's a real self-motivating character, always geeing himself up on the pitch.

I think that's one of the reasons we were so successful in the second half of the season: we covered the absences of regular players better than any of our rivals. In the past, I often felt the squad lacked genuine depth. After Christmas – once players had settled down – we had that strength in reserve. Look at the number of times David Platt came off the bench. Most teams would love to have someone of his ability and experience in the side, let alone among the subs. Stephen Hughes showed his value, as a starting player and as a sub. I was delighted for him, because he came through Arsenal's youth ranks like I did, and I'm always pleased to see home-grown players doing well.

What about our famous defence – the 'golden oldies' in front of 'Safe Hands' Seaman? I remember the FA Cup tie at Middlesbrough, when Boro piled on the pressure after Merse scored. The way Bouldy coped with that, you'd have thought he was twenty-five, not thirty-five. Bouldy, Lee Dixon and Nigel Winterburn are all the same. They have this fantastic appetite for the game and determination to succeed.

Martin Keown's pace has given us something extra too. He was outstanding after he came back from injury. Was it really sixteen years ago that we first started playing together in Arsenal's youth team?!

Ray Parlour was very unlucky not to go to France '98. He made huge strides. He attacked and defended with massive energy, went past people and set up loads of chances. He's always been capable of scoring as well, and he proved that too.

Patrick Vieira was a big influence in midfield. His partnership with Manu was hugely effective in the second half of the season. He's provided the link between defence and attack we've probably lacked since Paul Davis in the 1991 Championship team. And at twenty-two, there's so much more he can achieve.

Dennis deserved every award that came to him. He opened the season in sublime form. The way he conjured up those goals at Southampton, Leicester and Chelsea was something else. He was majestic on the run-in too. Barnsley at Oakwell was a potentially tricky match, but after Dennis had manufactured a goal out of nothing, we were always in control. It was such a shame that he had to miss the end of the season because of that hamstring injury. It would have meant so much to him to have played against Everton and at Wembley. But he's at the peak of his game now – probably physically stronger than I've ever seen him – and I'm sure he'll have a lot more to offer in the new season.

I was watching from the sidelines when Wrighty had to limp off for England against Morocco. That hamstring injury, which kept him out of France '98, was a cruel blow to someone who's such a fantastic enthusiast. He plays with his heart on his sleeve and his achievement in breaking the club scoring record was phenomenal.

Then I have to mention Matthew Upson. Football-wise, he reminds me of myself as a teenager: someone who's eager to learn and totally determined to succeed. I can't say any better than that I see him as my long-term successor.

Most Arsenal successes have been built around a nucleus of home-grown players. In that sense, the 1998 Double was different because only Martin, Ray, Hughesy and myself rose through the youth ranks. I know that flow of players is something M. Wenger wants to develop again.

I think it's great for the club that so many 'Arsenal men' are on the coaching and youth development staff. That ensures continuity and respect for the club's traditions. I was delighted when Don Howe came back as head of youth coaching, because he has so much knowledge to offer. Liam Brady was one of Arsenal's all-time greats, and – judging by the way the youngsters won the first-ever FA Premier Youth League title – he's already making an impact as head of youth development; assisted by another ex-Gunners player, David Court. George Armstrong does a great job with the reserves, pushing young players on, and helping experienced players keep fit or get back into action. I remember how helpful he was to me when I made my 'comebacks' last season.

Pat Rice is Arsenal through and through. He's been a big aid to M. Wenger. Apart from a few brief years at Watford he's spent all his adult life at Highbury and that shines out.

Over the last few years, I've spent rather longer than I'd have liked with Gary Lewin. That's because I've needed treatment more often than I'd have liked! Gary was once an Arsenal trainee goalkeeper. Now he's one of the finest physios around.

Which brings me to Arsène Wenger. He gained the players' confidence very quickly after he arrived. You can see on the pitch, the way we've responded to him. He's very shrewd. He knows when to listen and when to command. He knows when to make changes and when to leave well alone. He also knows what he wants and backs those he thinks can deliver it. He supported young players like Nicolas and Chris when people outside Highbury didn't realise their value. He supported me all the way when I needed to sort out my own injury worries around Christmas time. He backed new signings like Marc and Manu before everyone else fully appreciated them. He lets us go out and do our stuff. We play a much more open game now. Sure, we want to be solid when the other team have the ball – but our real focus is on causing the opposition problems.

It says a lot for the players' professionalism that we reacted to the home defeats against Liverpool and Blackburn by trying to sort things out among ourselves. It says a lot for M. Wenger, too, that he encouraged frank discussion and was prepared to listen to the things we said. He's not a man who shouts – but we all know when he has a point to make. He was such a calm figure when the pressure was at its height. He was totally focused on the next match alone. That transmitted itself to all the players: 'one game at a time' became our motto. I've never known a more focused group of players. That was crucial to our success.

One of M. Wenger's biggest achievements – and ours – has been to make Arsenal popular. I never thought I'd say that. Too often in the past, we've been damned with faint praise. In 1989 and 1991 we played dynamic football to win the Championship. In 1993, we pulled off the first-ever FA Cup and Coca-Cola Cup double. The following year we won the Cup-Winners' Cup against the odds. But we never received the acclaim we received in May. It was a somewhat strange – but nice – feeling to have people queuing up to say how much they enjoyed watching us. I hope that will long continue.

The Highbury crowd got behind us too, in a way I've rarely experienced. I'll never forget the second half against Derby, when we led 1–0. It seemed to go on for ever. In the dressing room afterwards, we all talked about the fans, singing all the way through the second half, doing their bit to help us on the way to glory. The scenes after the Everton game were amazing. So were the crowds who greeted us on our parade to Islington town hall on 17 May. I enjoyed every minute.

The next question is: how do we follow the Double? Obviously we want to win more trophies in 1998–99. I know from past experience how hard it is to retain the Championship when all the other clubs have a special reason for raising their game against you. That will be a big test. So will the Champions League. In the last two seasons, we've been hugely disappointed to go out of the UEFA Cup in the first round. We have some time to make up in Europe, although the English fixture list doesn't help. I never make rash forecasts, but I know M. Wenger wants to strengthen the squad even further. And I know how much we want to succeed – in England and Europe – in 1998–99.

In the meantime, this book is a treasury of memories of one of the greatest seasons in Arsenal's famous history. I hope you enjoy it.

ARSENAL F.C.
Double Winners
1997/98
ARRIVA
ARSENAL F.C.
Double
Winners
1997/98
ARSENAL
DOUBLE
WINNERS
1998

CELEBRATION

'Four months is a long time in football . . .' The speaker was Pat Rice, Arsène Wenger's assistant. The date was 16 May, the scene was Wembley. Arsenal had just started celebrating their second Double – emulating the feat of the 1971 side. The pace of Marc Overmars and Nicolas Anelka had destroyed Newcastle 2–0 in the FA Cup final, and the red-and-white half of north London was ready to party. Next morning an estimated 200,000 people turned out to cheer the Gunners as they paraded their trophies in an open-top bus from Highbury to Islington town hall.

A fortnight earlier, the stadium had revelled in its own carnival when Arsenal demolished Everton 4–0 to win the club's eleventh Championship. Supporters queued eagerly in the streets for title T-shirts and blow-up replicas of the Championship trophy. The souvenir programme sold out an hour before kick-off. The stadium was a sea of flags. The fans ran through their repertoire of songs. Everton were negative, but they were bit players in Arsenal's piece of theatre.

If the crowd – or players – had nerves, they were settled after six minutes. Tony Adams jumped with Slaven Bilic for a corner, and the Everton defender headed into his own net. Two flying individual goals by Marc Overmars killed off Everton. If those goals were symbolic of 'new Arsenal' then the last was the best of 'old Arsenal' – with a little help from Wenger. He'd encouraged his defenders to show their technique, and this was a sublime moment. Steve Bould played a delicate chip through the Everton defence – any midfielder would have been proud of it – and there was Adams, galloping clear to crash a left-foot shot past Thomas Myrhe. The celebrations in the ground, Avenell Road, then in north London's pubs, ran long into the night.

Meanwhile, Wenger entered the press conference to a round of spontaneous applause; some of it from writers who'd questioned only four months before, whether the Frenchman could succeed in England.

The open-topped team bus draws up outside Islington town hall.

'I've had to keep my emotions inside,' he began. 'Now I can say how proud I feel – very proud of what we've done. To win ten games in a row, and not to lose since December, that was magnificent and I am proud to be the first foreign manager to win the Championship. I didn't expect this at the start of the season because we had so many new players in the squad. But the team's spirit has been the real star – and when we won at Manchester United everyone began to believe we could be champions.'

With the pressure off, Arsenal – including eight changes – lost 0–4 at Liverpool the following Wednesday, then went down to Dwight Yorke's cheeky penalty in their final league game at Aston Villa. Villa captain Gareth Southgate felt the Gunners had eased off since the title was wrapped up, but said: 'If they'd needed to get a result, they'd have gone up a gear.'

So the Gunners went up a gear at Wembley. Overmars sprinted on to Manu Petit's pass to put Arsenal ahead. Then, after Alan Shearer had hit a post, Anelka raced on to Ray Parlour's through ball and fired a stinging cross-shot beyond Shay Given.

'Shearer's shot against the post was a turning point,' reflected Wenger. 'It would have been terrible if we'd lost, because who knows when we'll have another chance to win the Double? Then Nicolas scored, and I knew we were OK. I've won the cup now in three different countries – France, Japan and England – but never the Double. I felt proud to have done so well for Arsenal, and satisfy all the people at the club who had confidence in me.' It was a magical end to a season that for weeks threatened to tail off into disappointment and disillusion.

Tony Adams celebrates scoring the fourth goal against Everton as Arsenal secure the Premiership title.

Patrick Vieira and Manu Petit in the dressing room with the FA Cup.

The 1971 Double was an unlikely triumph at the time. Indeed, the Double only became an issue after Arsenal saw off Stoke in the FA Cup semi-final replay. It was the same in 1998, after the semi-final victory over Wolves. Even then, the race with Manchester United was expected to continue to the very end. The decisive day was probably 18 April, when Arsenal hammered Wimbledon 5–0 to go top, after Newcastle had held United 1–1 at Old Trafford. It was a remarkable turn-round for Wenger's Gunners, written off early in the new year – probably even more remarkable than the 1971 side's triumph.

Rice played right-back in that team. Managed by Bertie Mee and coached by Don Howe, they pursued Leeds throughout a gruelling season, clinching the title only with Ray Kennedy's eighty-seventh minute goal at Tottenham in their final league game. Frank McLintock, inspirational skipper in 1971, noted the similarities between then and 1998. 'We were seven points behind Leeds, which was almost identical to the thirteen Arsenal were behind Manchester United, because it was only two points for a win then. We came through with twenty-five points out of the last twenty-eight possible. It was an extra-ordinary run-in from our point of view. Arsène's team did exactly the same, coming from behind and finding great form at the right time.'

In January 1971, few even contemplated an Arsenal Double – even if the Gunners were pushing Leeds, English football's team of the age, at the top. McLintock's team had to bounce back from the occasional disaster, like the 0–5 defeat at Stoke. But they never had to cope with the mid-season worries that threatened to engulf Wenger's squad.

In January 1998, anyone who backed Arsenal to win the Double would have been considered a candidate for the men in white coats. The Gunners had lost four games out of six between 1 November and 13 December, when the 1–3 capitulation to Blackburn had roused even the taciturn Wenger to anger. Arsenal stood fifth in the league, way behind the leaders Manchester United. Wenger later admitted that he wondered if the Gunners still had a chance of reaching the Champions League, let alone entering as title holders. 'At that stage, I thought it was over,' he said.

The Gunners had just scraped through a third round FA Cup replay on penalties at Port Vale – a struggling Nationwide Division One club – after Vale ground out a goalless draw at Highbury. Only the Coca-Cola Cup, in which Arsenal had just won 2–1 at West Ham in the quarter-final, seemed to offer hope of a trophy.

The rumour factory was working overtime. There was an alleged split in the dressing room between the English players and the Frenchmen Wenger had imported. Tony Adams had just returned from a clinic in the south of France, his career threatened by a long-term ankle injury. Ian Wright, involved in a public argument with supporters, after the Blackburn defeat, was hurt at Port Vale and wouldn't start in the league again until May. As then eighteen-year-old Nicolas Anelka stepped up to start Premier League games for the first time, supporters wondered why Wenger had sold John Hartson and Paul Merson. Meanwhile, the Gunners had amassed one of the worst disciplinary records in the Premier League.

Patrick Barclay wrote in the *Sunday Telegraph*: 'Gone are the warmly reassuring days of autumn, when Highbury's horizon seemed limitless. Out of Europe, and slipping behind in the Premiership race, Arsenal must take both domestic cups seriously, and that, in the often ridiculously demanding world of the English game, verges on a crisis.' Mark Lawrenson in the *Mirror* had been even blunter. 'Arsenal fans are beginning to question Wenger's tactics and ability, for the first time since he arrived at the club.'

That Saturday, David Seaman broke a finger in the 2–2 draw at Coventry – and Patrick Vieira was sent off. Could things get any worse?

No one realised it at the time, but these were the stirrings of a remarkable run. The draw at Coventry was Arsenal's fourth league game unbeaten. There would be fourteen more in that sequence including thirteen wins, climaxing on that festive afternoon against Everton. Arsenal's eternal back four, strengthened by Martin Keown's pace, were the rock. The Gunners conceded just two goals in those fourteen matches. That strength was vital on the road to Wembley too, as the Gunners edged through at Middlesbrough and Crystal Palace and won on penalties at West Ham.

But '1–0 to the Arsenal' became a familiar cry again, as between 26 December and 3 May, only Chelsea – on an emotional Coca-Cola Cup semi-final night at Stamford Bridge – beat Arsenal.

Reasons for the Gunners' resurgence could be traced back to December. After the defeats by Liverpool and Blackburn, Wenger called team meetings, to which Adams was an influential contributor. It was no accident that Arsenal's growing solidity coincided with Patrick Vieira and Manu Petit taking more defensive responsibility, to stop attackers running at the back four. The French pair finished the season as two of the Premiership's most influential players, creative and destructive. Those meetings were soon followed by the squad's Christmas party, at which all the players came together – an important step on the path to the team spirit praised by Wenger.

Arsenal finally swept to the title with a flourish. Dennis Bergkamp, Footballer of the Year, was majestic against Blackburn, Wimbledon and Barnsley, matching his outstanding early season form. Overmars and Ray Parlour, in their contrasting styles, were hugely effective wide men. Then there were the players who stepped in. As Bob Wilson pointed out, Arsenal's squad players contributed far more effectively than their counterparts at Manchester. David Platt turned his vast experience to good use. Alex Manninger was a revelation, deputising for Seaman. Stephen Hughes scored vital goals against Chelsea and earned himself a five-year contract. Chris Wreh, of the somersault celebration, hit even more vital goals, like the winner at Bolton and the shot that beat Wolves in the semi-final. Gilles Grimandi's volley against Crystal Palace kept the Gunners' run going when they were hit by injuries. Anelka learned with every game and broke into the France side. 'In the end, we played as a team, and everyone chipped in,' said Adams.

Arsène Wenger addresses the crowd after the team has paraded the trophies from the stadium to Islington town hall.

Wenger and Adams set the tone for the run-in, focusing relentlessly on whichever game was next – whatever was said in Manchester, or by their opponents. As Wenger summed up: 'What the team have done since December has been incredible. Our tactical organisation improved. Our youngsters improved, and our spirit got better and better.'

The Gunners' success was even more impressive because they defied the odds to achieve it. But then, as Rice said, 'When did Arsenal ever do anything the easy way?!'

EXPECTATIONS

The Moray Arms in Finsbury Park is more than just an Arsenal pub; it's more like a shrine to the Gunners. Its regulars couldn't wait for the start of the 1997–98 season. One of them is Arsenal Ladies successful manager Terry Howard. He summed up: 'After all the turmoil of the previous summer, we could see something good being built. Arsène Wenger had strengthened the squad and we expected Arsenal to be serious contenders again.'

Such high hopes were echoed throughout the red-and-white half of north London. Supporters looked back on the previous season and thought, 'If only . . .' If only Arsenal had taken home points against title rivals Manchester United, Newcastle and Liverpool they could have been champions, instead of finishing third and missing out on the Champions League to Newcastle on goal difference.

Since taking over on 28 September 1996, Arsène Wenger had restored stability after Bruce Rioch's departure. He had won the trust of the players. As Pat Rice said: 'He has tremendous strength of character. He doesn't threaten people. He lets you know what he expects, but he does it in a way that shows respect – and he gets that respect back from the dressing room.'

Wenger had also firmly established himself with the fans. One reason for their optimism was his success in his first season. The other was the seven signings Arsenal had made. Said Wenger: 'In England, maybe more than anywhere else, a manager is judged on the players he recruits. I remember, when we lost a game last season the fans would tell me to go out and buy someone!'

'Arsène has an eye for a player,' said Rice. 'Signing Patrick Vieira was one of the coups of last season. As far as our fans were concerned, Patrick had come from nowhere. Now he's a big hero.'

That summer, Wenger had made two important decisions that went hand-in-hand. Arsenal would switch from Rioch's 3–5–2 to the Frenchman's favoured 4–4–2 – and the Gunners needed more penetration on the

Manu Petit on his debut in the pre-season game at St Albans.

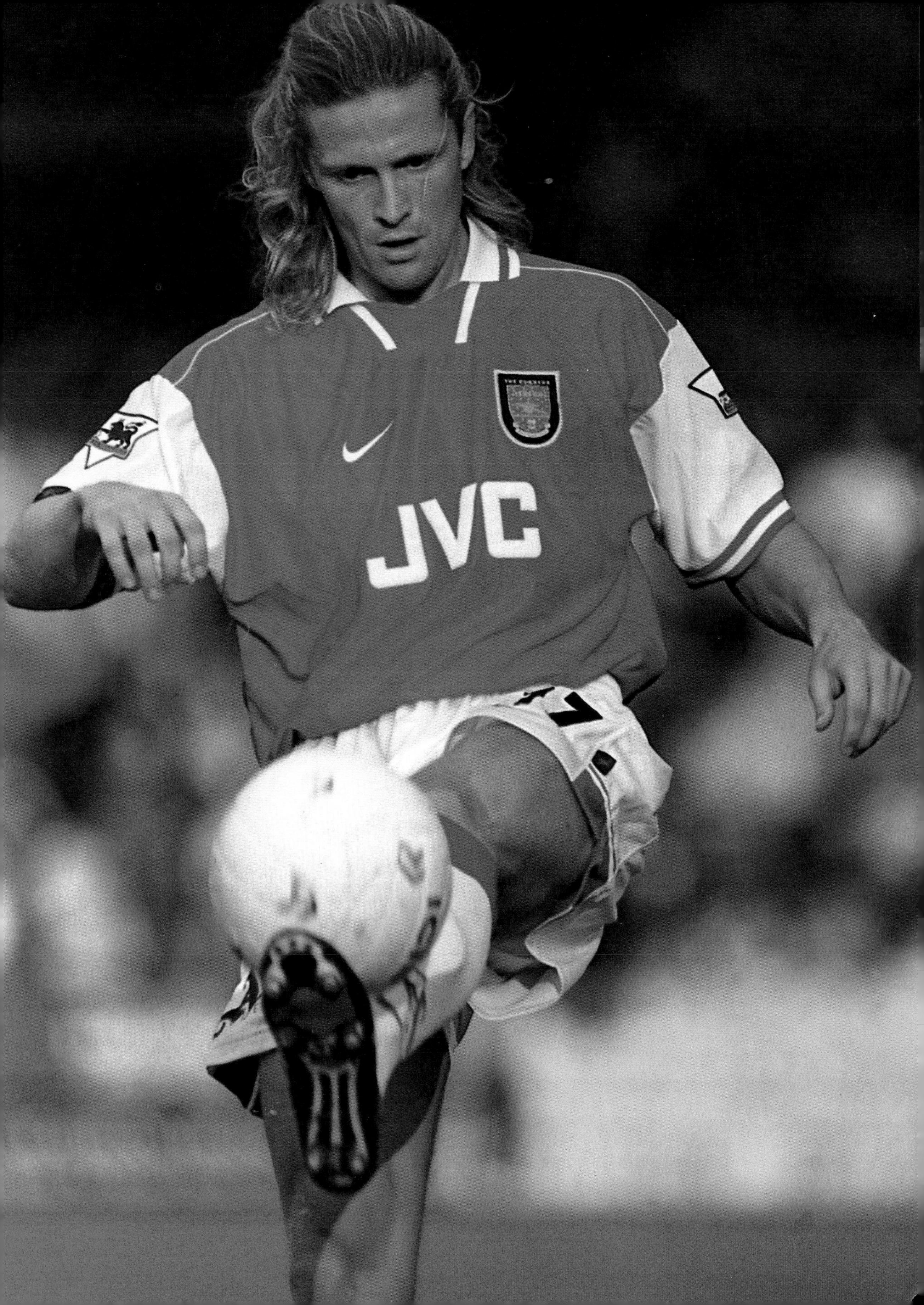
JVC

Marc Overmars takes on the Norwich defence.

flanks. 'We needed more offensive power, especially in the big games,' said Wenger.

Enter Marc Overmars. The Holland winger was at the end of his contract with Ajax, and had decided to leave. 'We'd won many trophies while everyone enjoyed playing together,' explained Overmars. 'Last season, though, the spirit was not right. We didn't reach our potential because players weren't happy to play for each other.'

The contest was between Arsenal – who already included Overmars's old Ajax colleague Dennis Bergkamp – and ambitious Spanish club Seville. But there were queries about Overmars's fitness. How well had he recovered from the serious knee injury that kept him out of Euro 96? Wenger moved fast. 'I think the whole of Europe wondered if Marc was finished because of his knee,' said Wenger. 'Marc was very upset about the rumours. I had to make a quick decision – and I was confident he'd get through an English season.'

That signing lifted the whole club. 'I hoped we'd have players coming in, and they've come,' said Rice, who predicted: 'Marc can unlock defences. His pace is electric. He'll make a big impact.'

Wenger also signed twenty-year-old left winger Luis Boa Morte – one of Portugal's stars in the annual Toulon tournament – from Sporting Lisbon. 'A turning point in my career,' said Boa Morte. Overmars on the right, and Boa Morte on the left – that was one of Wenger's options. Ray Parlour's performances would have something to say about that. But Boa Morte was essentially a player for the future.

So were Matthew Upson and Alex Manninger. England Under-18 centre-back Upson arrived from Luton. Pressed into service to deputise for Nigel Winterburn during the pre-season games, Upson looked calm and composed – despite his farcical sending-off in the friendly against PSV in Eindhoven, when the referee mixed him up with Boa Morte! Chief scout Steve Rowley had spotted Manninger, then just nineteen, keeping goal for Grazer AK. Bob Wilson quickly confirmed Manninger's immense potential. The ruddy-cheeked Austrian would play a vital part in Arsenal's success, standing in for David Seaman in the New Year.

Alberto Mendez – Nuremburg-born son of Spanish parents – was plucked from obscurity with SC Feucht in the Bavarian Regional League. He was the unlucky one. Ankle surgery would rip the heart out of his season, after he'd made his first-team debut. Then there were the men from Wenger's old club, Monaco – Manu Petit and Gilles Grimandi. Both had played in Monaco's 1997 French Championship side. The left-footed Petit had switched from defence to midfield with great effect. Versatile Grimandi did a job anywhere along the back line. Petit soon showed his quality with a defence-splitting pass to Ian Wright when Arsenal won 2–1 at Wenger's hometown club, Strasbourg. As the season opened, a third ex-Monaco player took Wenger's summer signings to eight: Liberian international forward Chris Wreh, now a French national because of European Union employment law.

The heart of the team remained. Seaman in goal; the legendary back four: Lee Dixon, Adams, Steve Bould and Nigel Winterburn, supplemented by Martin Keown, once he'd recovered from his shoulder injury in Le Tournoi. In midfield, Arsenal could call on Vieira's huge promise and David Platt's experience. Up front were Wright – with Cliff Bastin's Arsenal scoring record in his sights – and the blessed Dennis Bergkamp.

Alex Manninger saves a shot in the friendly at Leyton Orient.

Stephen Hughes had shown he was ready for Premier football. Nicolas Anelka was beginning to settle in. There was only one cloud on the horizon: the sale of Paul Merson to Middlesbrough. That raised eyebrows among supporters who regarded Merse as a Highbury fixture. But the fans were prepared to give Wenger the benefit of the doubt.

Merson is philosophical now. 'Arsène told me he'd be playing 4–4–2 and it would be a problem fitting me in,' said Merson. 'In a way he did me a favour, letting me go, because I've found a new lease of life at Boro. The way the Arsenal team has developed since, I can't see a place for me in the formation. I could have been sitting on the bench as a sub all season. But Arsène gave me the story straight, and – looking back – it was the best thing.'

While Wenger was re-shaping the first team squad, Liam Brady was working to strengthen the Gunners' youth set-up. Arsenal were to field two youth sides in 1997–98 – an Under-19 squad in the newly formed FA Premier Youth League, plus the South East Counties team. In came Don Givens and Neil Banfield as coaches, and Don Howe as head of youth coaching. Howe was the coaching brain behind the 1971 Double winners and the teams that reached Wembley three years running between 1978 and 1980. He had analysed youth coaching systems throughout Europe for the FA. Now Arsenal would benefit again from his experience. He was another investment for the future. As Rice said: 'Don is one of our best signings, because he has so much to teach.' It was a dramatic turn-round from the paralysis of the previous summer, and Rioch's departure five days before the start of the season.

But Wenger gave no hostages to fortune. He was bothered by Arsenal's number of suspensions. 'I have to improve our record without stifling our competitive spirit,' he said. He also wondered if all the changes he'd made would affect the continuity of the side. 'I'm pleased with what I've seen,' he

Ian Wright scores a spectacular overhead goal against Norwich.

said. 'The new players have worked hard to integrate. The other players have worked hard to adapt. But it's not easy to bring in so many new players – usually it's only two or three at this time of year – and change the structure of the team. I have taken a risk, which I hope will be justified.'

Then five days before the start of the season, on the anniversary of Rioch's untimely departure, the Gunners took Norwich apart 6–2 in a friendly at Carrow Road. Wright grabbed a hat trick, Bergkamp scored too. 'This was a performance of power and potential,' said Michael Hart in the *Evening Standard*. 'On this form, Arsenal can undoubtedly challenge for the Championship.'

After that win, Adams put that task into perspective. 'Don't ask me to forecast the title race,' he said. 'What I do know is that I'm more optimistic than I've been for a while. We have a big squad with quality players, and strength in depth. We can compete, no doubts. That's where mental toughness comes in. Anyone can talk. It's people who deliver under pressure who are successful.'

In the Moray Arms, they echoed every word.

FLYING START

'We've just seen the next champions of England,' said George Graham.

It was Arsenal's first game of the season, a 1–1 draw at Elland Road. 'Surely too early for predictions, George?' asked a journalist who'd known Graham well at Highbury – and remembered his horror of making rash forecasts. 'No,' replied Graham. 'I think Arsenal will win it once they settle down, because they have so many good individuals now, an embarrassment of riches.'

Graham's prediction proved amazingly prophetic – but there was another agenda involved. Graham had never been able to spend more than £15 million on new players in one summer, let alone bring high-price, high-wage stars like Dennis Bergkamp and Marc Overmars to Highbury.

Overmars, Gilles Grimandi and Manu Petit made their Premiership debuts. Graham sat David Hopkin on Patrick Vieira, but the Gunners still created chances. Ian Wright could have had a first-half hat trick. He fired Arsenal ahead from an acute angle with his most difficult chance. Jimmy Floyd Hasselbaink equalised three minutes before half time. The balance turned, as Leeds chased a winner.

'A colossus,' Graham used to call Steve Bould. With Lee Dixon injured, Martin Keown out for the first half of the season after his injury in Le Tournoi and Tony Adams suspended, he had to be, as the Gunners weathered heavy pressure. Bould picked up a knock at Elland Road which kept him out of the Monday night win over Coventry. Arsenal fielded a back four reading Remi Garde, Grimandi, Scott Marshall and Nigel Winterburn. But the Sky Blues were never a threat. Wright netted both goals in a 2–0 win, which took him to 177. Only two to go, to beat Cliff Bastin's Arsenal record.

Southampton, injury-hit and making a terrible start, were next, at The Dell. Overmars shot Arsenal in front with his first Premiership goal, after twenty minutes. Neil Maddison levelled for the Saints. Then

Dennis Bergkamp scores Arsenal's third at Southampton.

10

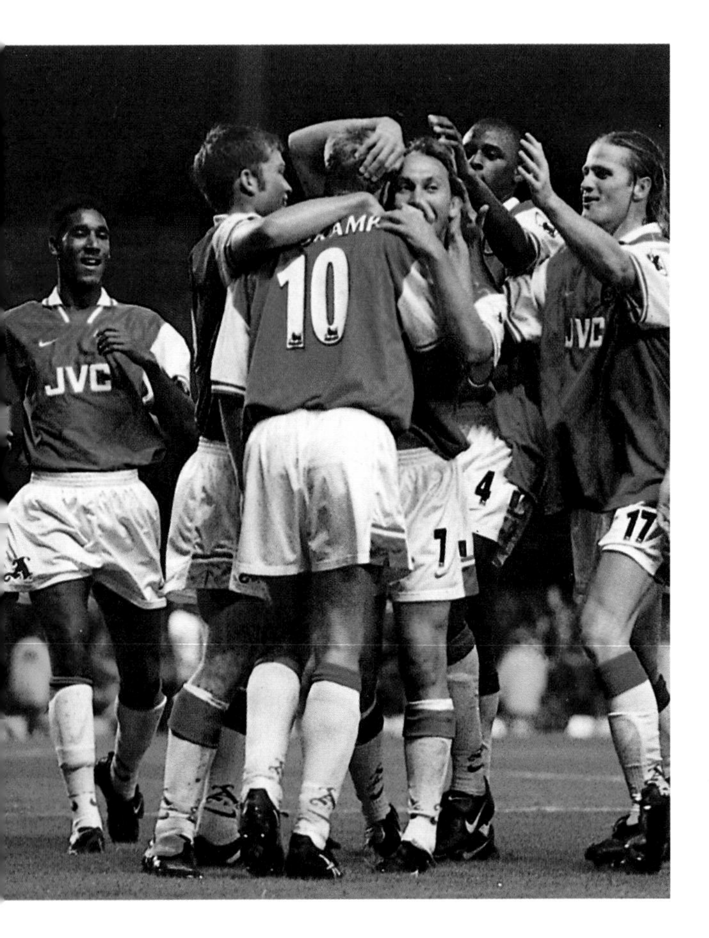

Dennis Bergkamp is mobbed by his team-mates after completing his hat trick against Leicester City.

Bergkamp, in mercurial form, scored twice in the second half to clinch a 3–1 win.

The midweek game at Leicester was a Bergkamp masterclass. But Arsenal gained only one point from a 3–3 draw, when they should have had three in the bag. The Dutchman scored a majestic hat trick, all dramatic finishes of skill and power. His third goal, subsequently named BBC's Goal of the Season, will live forever in the minds of those who saw it. He lobbed the ball over Matt Elliott, controlled it with one touch, then crashed a shot past Kasey Keller from a tight angle. 'What can you say about a hat trick of that quality?' said Tony Adams, who was still missing because of injury. 'I'm just glad I don't have to mark him!'

But, as Adams acknowledged, Arsenal's problems had been at the other end. 'We can't concede goals like we did in the closing stages at Leicester,' he said. Bergkamp had given Arsenal a two-goal lead. Emile Heskey pulled one back six minutes from time. The excitement erupted in injury time. Elliott levelled for Leicester. Bergkamp made it 3–2 to Arsenal. Steve Walsh equalised again. The atmosphere was highly charged. Finally, there was a fracas at the end of the match which landed Wright and Walsh before the FA.

Arsène Wenger was more concerned about the way the Gunners dropped two points. 'I was very disappointed with their second goal, because we gave away a stupid corner and didn't deal with the rebounds properly,' he said. 'Leicester showed good spirit, but Dennis's third goal should have been the winner.' It was a theme that would recur in the next few weeks.

Arsenal annihilated Tottenham in the north London derby – and drew 0–0. Spurs came for a point and got it, despite having Justin Edinburgh sent off for a second bookable offence. 'We should have been three up at half time,' said Wenger, after Bergkamp, Overmars and Wright had all rattled the Tottenham woodwork.

Wright broke Bastin's record with a hat trick in the 4–1 win over Bolton, after Alan Thompson had the temerity to put Wanderers in front. As Wright celebrated his first goal, he popped off his shirt to reveal a Nike vest bearing the inscription '179'. 'I definitely think we're going to win something this year,' said Wright. 'I can see so much potential in the squad.' Chelsea were London's other leading team when Arsenal went to Stamford Bridge. Bergkamp was magnificent again, twice beating fellow Dutchman Ed de Goey to put Arsenal 2–1 up, after Gustavo Poyet had struck for Chelsea. 'He'd have had two more, but for De Goey,' said Adams. The captain was back too. But these weren't the mean Gunners of Graham's years. The Blues went straight to the other end and made it 2–2 through Gianfranco Zola, after a mix-up between Adams and David Seaman.

As Wenger admitted, the sending-off of Frank Leboeuf for a second yellow card was a crucial factor. It gave Wenger a tricky choice. 'I had to decide whether to bring on more strikers, or to back our team on the pitch to exploit the extra space.' Wenger backed the team on the pitch.

Nigel Winterburn caught out all the photographers with his late winner against Chelsea.

The winner came from an unlikely source: Nigel Winterburn, who cracked a stunning shot that would have delighted even Roberto Carlos. 'I was so happy to see the ball end up in the back of the net because it was such an important goal,' said Winterburn. 'To give away a silly goal after we'd gone 2–1 up was very frustrating, but after my shot went in, the celebrations were a way of letting the tension out.'

Amid the joy, there were worries. For all their flowing football, the Gunners had almost let Chelsea back in the match. Bookings were piling up too, especially for Bould, and Bergkamp. Referees rarely gave the Dutchman the protection he deserved, but they were quick to reach for the yellow card when he retaliated or questioned a decision. 'Dennis is at his peak now,' said Wenger. 'He's a fantastic player to watch and I'm delighted he's in the spotlight, because I don't think he's always received the recognition he's deserved. I still can't understand why he wasn't accepted in Italy – but that has been Arsenal's gain.'

West Ham were swept aside on Wednesday. John Hartson, back for his first game since moving to E13, left an impression on Winterburn but none on the Arsenal net. Bergkamp stroked the Gunners into a twelfth-minute lead, then three goals in six minutes just before half time – two by Overmars and a Wright penalty – killed the game. 'I'd say that performance was sixty per cent of what we're aiming for,' said Adams, with no tongue in cheek.

But the doubts about Arsenal's solidity surfaced again at Everton, struggling at the foot of the table. Wright and Overmars gave the Gunners a two-goal half-time cushion. Two unknown youngsters, Michael Ball and Danny Cadamarteri, hauled Everton level by eleven minutes after half time. 'We should never have let them back in it,' said Adams. 'It wasn't one of our better performances. They controlled the first twenty minutes, and the first twenty minutes of the second half.'

Highbury was dancing again the following Saturday when the Gunners overwhelmed Barnsley 5–0. Seaman had to pull off two flying saves though, before Bergkamp started the rout with a wicked curling shot. Bergkamp again, the revitalised Ray Parlour, David Platt and Wright finished the job.

Then the Premier goals dried up. At Crystal Palace, Bergkamp ran into a young Icelander called Hermann Hreidarsson, who blocked, tugged, obstructed and generally frustrated the Dutchman. Who did referee Steve Dunn book? Bergkamp – his fifth yellow card, which earned him a suspension. 'I'll have to try to get used to the bumps and bruises,' said Bergkamp ruefully.

'I was bothered by Dennis's booking,' said Wenger. 'He is not an unfair player. But he needs referees to protect him against unfair challenges.'

Wenger thought Arsenal should have had a penalty when Luis Boa Morte (deputising for the injured Overmars) was felled. Yet he admitted, 'We didn't dominate as I'd hoped and we didn't create enough chances.'

Bergkamp looked subdued on his last appearance before the ban, a goalless draw against Aston Villa at Highbury. 'We needed to get more crosses in,' said Adams. But Arsenal didn't just drop two points. They also lost Manu Petit to suspension – red-carded by referee Paul Durkin after laying hands on the man in black.

It had been an exhilarating start: twelve Premier games unbeaten. As Adams said, 'We have individuals who can turn games even when we're under pressure, and we don't just rely on Wrighty for goals any more.' It would have been even better, had Arsenal hung on to their leads at Leicester and Everton. Arsenal had played some wonderful flowing football, yet at times looked vulnerable. As the *Evening Standard*'s Michael Hart pointed out: 'They don't get behind the ball like they used to.'

Now Bergkamp was suspended. Bould and Petit would soon join him. Wright had hit a lean spell after breaking Bastin's record, and plenty of problems were waiting to be solved.

Marc Overmars shoots past Ludek Miklosko to score against West Ham.

179
just done it.

WRIGHTY

It was just a case of *when*, not *if* . . . Ian Wright started 1997–98 needing five goals to beat Cliff Bastin's Arsenal scoring record. Wright already held the club records for the most goals in the League Cup and in Europe. Bastin, the flying left winger of the 1930s, never had the chance to play in such competitions. Wright got off to a great start, shooting the Gunners ahead in the 1–1 draw at Leeds on the opening day of the season. Twice he beat Steve Ogrizovic in one-on-ones, to see off Coventry 2–0 in the opening league game at Highbury. 'I definitely think we're going to win something this season,' forecast Wright. 'We have players capable of winning the Championship.'

Dennis Bergkamp took centre stage in the 3–1 win at Southampton and the 3–3 draw at Leicester, then the woodwork denied Wright against Tottenham. Three games without a goal: were thoughts of the record affecting Wright? 'I want the record, but it won't mean anything unless we've won something at the end of the season,' he replied. 'My goals have to mean something to the team and I'm looking long beyond the record.'

Ian Wright celebrates his second goal which took him on to 179 goals - a new Arsenal record.

But the tension was building. As Tony Adams said: 'I hope Wrighty breaks the record as soon as possible, so that all the hype can die down.' He did, with a hat trick against Bolton, on 13 September. Alan Thompson put Bolton in front. Then Wrighty's treble, plus one from Ray Parlour, made it 4–1 for the Gunners. 'We knew all about the Arsenal record,' said Bolton manager Colin Todd. 'We just wish he hadn't chosen us as the victims!'

Ian Chadband wrote in the *Sunday Times*: 'Who writes Ian Wright's script? The irrepressible one was not just content with breaking Cliff Bastin's venerable record. No, his sense of theatre demanded that he mark the occasion by completing a splendid hat trick. Highbury's deafening salute was as affectionate as it was ecstatic. When he was taken off, eight minutes from the end, the grand old stadium rose as one. It was typical Wright: industry and sheer class in equal measure – one of his specials to equal the record, one your granny could have scored to break it, and finally a master-class in finishing to put the seal on a historic afternoon.'

Wright, ever aware of a photo opportunity, wore a Nike T-shirt emblazoned: '179 Just done it' beneath his Arsenal shirt. Indeed, he was so pleased at converting Bergkamp's through ball to wipe out Thompson's early goal, and equal Bastin's record, that he pulled up his shirt to give fans and photographers a sneak preview. After his second, tapping in a rebound off Bolton keeper Keith Branagan, he could celebrate in earnest. 'I was happy before I put it in. I'll never score an easier one!' The third was the climax, a first-time twenty-yard volley past Branagan. Chairman Peter Hill-Wood presented Wright with a club award before the next home game, against West Ham, when he dispatched a penalty in the Gunners' 4–0 win.

George Graham signed Wright from Crystal Palace in September 1991. The £2.5 million fee was an Arsenal record at the time. Typically, Wright scored on his debut, in a 1–1 League Cup draw at Leicester, then hit a hat trick on his Arsenal league debut in a 4–0 win at Southampton. He won the Golden Shoe that season, pipping Gary Lineker on the last day, thanks to another hat trick against Southampton. Michael Hart of the *Evening Standard* accurately analysed Wright's qualities: 'He has a distinctive, arresting style. He's a player of speed and strength. But the beauty of his game is that he makes goalscoring look so easy.'

Wright was thirty-three when he broke Bastin's record. He came late into top-class football; he was twenty-one when Palace signed him from Greenwich Borough. He jokes, even now, that he retains characteristics of the Sunday morning pub player. 'I remember working on building sites before I got into the pro game,' said Wright. 'The frustrations and knock-backs of those early years have been key factors in keeping me going.' Graham recognised that, years ago. 'Ian is a great athlete and he has this terrific hunger to succeed. That's why I always thought he'd score goals at an age when most top strikers have packed up.' 'He has such wonderful enthusiasm,' said Arsène Wenger. 'He loves scoring goals for Arsenal. He keeps himself in very good condition and he is still so very quick over the vital first few yards.'

Wright's instincts have frequently got him into trouble with referees and Lancaster Gate. Bruce Rioch, for one, was keen that Wright should improve his disciplinary record. Last season, Wright even saw a 'rage counsellor' to try to cool his aggression on the pitch. 'I regret there have been some embarrassing moments, which have given people a chance to criticise me and the club,' he admitted. Maybe you can't have one without the other. Take away the aggression that fuels Wright's desire and you remove one of the qualities that make him Arsenal's record-breaker. 'I live on the edge of several emotions,' he said. 'I'm really a softy, but with a streak of devil.'

It was typical Wright too, that for his 'One2One' television commercial, he chose

Ian Wright hits the equaliser against Bolton to draw level with Cliff Bastin.

Martin Luther King as the person he'd most like to have spoken to. Other celebrities in the series played safe by picking showbiz or sporting heroes. But Wright has never favoured soft options. Wright's early heroes were Britain's first black football stars, like Laurie Cunningham and Cyrille Regis. Now he has become an inspiration to aspiring young black sports people. That makes him proud: a feat to complement his achievements for the Gunners.

Inevitably, the debate raged: what was Wright's best goal for Arsenal? John Cross, once the *Islington Gazette*'s Arsenal expert, expressed a popular view: 'Only Ian Wright could upstage a team-mate who'd just scored a hat trick. But that's what Wrighty did when he scored my own personal favourite of his many wonderful goals for Arsenal. It was on 27 December 1993, at Swindon Town. Kevin Campbell had already scored three as Arsenal led 3–0 in the dying seconds of a one-sided Premiership match. But, as only Wright can, he picked up the ball thirty-five yards outside the box, spotted Swindon keeper Fraser Digby off his line, then unleashed a spectacular chip. The sheer audacity of the shot left the goalkeeper – and the crowd – stunned.'

But Wright had scored one he'd rank ahead of that: the second in a 2–0 win over Everton at Highbury in August 1993. Wright juggled the ball over Matt Jackson, then caught it as it came down, and gave Neville Southall no chance. 'People still talk to me about that goal,' said Wright. 'It wasn't my original intention to score like that. Jackson came across, but I was always a step ahead of him and I had time to chip Southall before Jackson's foot came across.'

Wright is an instinctive striker. Yet no one has more thoroughly studied videos of successful strikers and learned from them. Wright has learned a lot from 'the enemy' – goalkeepers – too. 'You need a good first touch to set you up,' said Wright. 'Then you have to look up and see what the goalkeeper is doing. At that stage, you need to be calm. I usually think the first thing that comes into my mind is the best option. The keeper is waiting for you to make a move, while you're waiting for him to make a move. So whoever has the most courage usually wins. I've always learned from the goalkeepers I've played with – Perry Suckling and Nigel Martyn at Palace; David Seaman with Arsenal and England. It helps in training, to have to produce something special to beat them.'

Wright's Highbury fans were willing him to make more history: to become the first Gunner to pass 200 goals. But that celebration against Bolton was to be the high point of Wright's season. After his penalty against West Ham, he scored at Everton and at home to Barnsley. Then he didn't net another league goal for two months, until he nodded home Dennis Bergkamp's centre for the winner at Newcastle. The tabloids who'd acclaimed him in September were writing of goal droughts. Wright had another photogenic answer. When he scored, he lifted his jersey to reveal another Nike T-shirt. This one was inscribed: 'At last!'

In between, Wright was one of England's heroes, playing a lone striker's role because of Alan Shearer's injury as Glenn Hoddle's team gained a goalless draw in Rome to qualify for France '98. So it was one of the saddest sights of the season to see Wright limp off early with a hamstring injury in England's friendly against Morocco in Casablanca, and out of contention for the World Cup finals.

Wright was suspended for the Christmas derby at Tottenham. He returned for the FA Cup tie against Port Vale and the home win over Leeds. Then, in the replay at Port Vale, he pulled a hamstring. That set a chain of injuries in motion. He played just twenty-two minutes as a sub against Chelsea on 8 February during the next fifteen weeks. Physio Gary Lewin explained: 'He had to overcome one problem after another. The first was the hamstring. Then he tore a cartilage in a training match. Following a surgical repair to that, he pulled a groin muscle in another training game.'

Wright's appeal was shown on his return. More than 4,000 watched him play sixty-one minutes for the Gunners' reserves against West Ham at Southend on 27 April. He came on for the last twenty minutes of the Championship carnival against Everton. But Paul Ince's 'tackle' forced Wright off at Liverpool three days later, and Wenger kept him on the bench at Wembley.

Ian Wright won't be short of offers when he finally hangs up his boots. His infectious personality makes him a television natural. He's already successfully hosted two chat shows for ITV. He even asked the actress Rosanna Arquette if there were any openings in Hollywood! But Wright will be chasing goals on the pitch for a while yet, though now for West Ham, the club he joined in July. Wherever he goes, however, Wright will always be fondly remembered by Arsenal fans, as a scoring phenomenon.

More celebrations as Ian Wright scores the second goal against Everton in 1993, the one he considers his best goal for the club.

reusch

OOPS!

So far, Arsenal's only disappointment had come in the UEFA Cup. Playing without the non-flying Dennis Bergkamp, the Gunners had gone down 0–1 to PAOK in Salonika. At Highbury, Bergkamp levelled on aggregate. But Arsenal couldn't break down a packed defence, and Zizis Vrizas's eighty-fifth minute breakaway goal took PAOK through.

Then, as November began, Arsenal's league challenge was about to stutter.

Bergkamp was suspended for the game at Derby on 1 November. Marc Overmars was injured. Arsenal, inspired by Patrick Vieira, dominated the first half but couldn't score. When Vieira was up-ended in the box, Ian Wright fired the penalty against the woodwork, and Nicolas Anelka headed the rebound over. At half time, Derby boss Jim Smith switched to a back three, pushed his full-backs on and moved Paulo Wanchope to attack Arsenal's right flank, where Lee Dixon had pressed forward in the opening half. Within a minute, Wanchope broke from the halfway line and curled a shot past David Seaman, via a slight deflection off Steve Bould's heel. Twenty minutes later, Nigel Winterburn's mis-kick presented Wanchope with Derby's second. Dean Sturridge made it 3–0 with a chip over Seaman. 'We needed to score while we were outplaying them,' said Adams, who admitted Arsenal had made defensive errors.

It wasn't the best way to approach a top-of-the-table clash with Manchester United, who'd thrashed Sheffield Wednesday 6–1 while the Gunners lost at Pride Park. United led Arsenal by four points. The media message was insistent throughout the week: Arsenal had to win, otherwise the title would slip away. Wenger smiled behind his glasses. He refused to entertain the hype or be drawn into psychological warfare with Alex Ferguson. 'I have more important things to be concerned about than words or mind games before such an important match,' he said. 'Last season we lost the Championship at home. Now we are stronger at home. It will be a

Peter Schmeichel is distraught at letting in the crucial goal at Highbury.

David Platt heads the winner against Manchester United.

good occasion to show we can beat United without Dennis.' Tony Adams was talking up an Arsenal revival. 'We have to put ourselves back on course and today is the perfect occasion. We couldn't have wished for bigger-name opponents to get us firing again.'

Manu Petit was suspended, but Overmars was fit again and the Gunners made a dream start. After seven minutes, Overmars's dribble unhinged the United defence and the ball fell to Anelka who tucked away a low shot. Twenty minutes later, Vieira blasted home a twenty-yarder – then celebrated so vigorously that he missed the next four league games because of a pulled muscle. United fought back. Teddy Sheringham, pulling off Arsenal's centre-back pairing of Adams and Gilles Grimandi, caused havoc. Striking from deep positions, he scored twice to level by half time. 'Sheringham is a very intelligent player,' said Wenger. 'We weren't well-positioned to deal with him.'

At half time Wenger, the disciple of 4–4–2, brought on Steve Bould for Vieira and switched to three at the back. It was a tactical master-stroke. 'We looked more solid and compact in the second half,' he said. 'United didn't really threaten us. I always felt we could score from a quick attack or a set piece.' Ray Parlour became ever more influential as Arsenal stepped up the pressure. As Michael Hart wrote in the *Evening Standard*: 'If Arsenal are to oust Manchester United as champions, then the resilience and tenacity demonstrated by the boy from Romford will be at least as important as the finer brush strokes from Highbury's expensive collection of French and Dutch masters.' With seven minutes left, Parlour's pass split United's defence. Wright timed his run to beat the offside trap, then centred for substitute Chris Wreh. Somehow Peter Schmeichel palmed round Wreh's close-range shot. Winterburn swung over the corner and David Platt, replacing Petit, outjumped everyone to head a dramatic winner.

'United are still the benchmark, still the team to beat, but this result has lifted us,' said Wright.

'Psychologically it was very important,' said Platt. 'It was effectively a six-pointer, even at this stage of the season. Just being one point behind United instead of seven banishes negative thoughts. We hadn't been playing particularly well, so this result gave us a boost. If we'd lost two games in a row, that would have been a big blow.' He added, 'United are still favourites for the title, but we have the quality and depth in our squad to challenge them.'

England's friendly against Cameroon meant a blank Premiership weekend. Then the Gunners travelled to Hillsborough. After a disastrous start to the season, the Sheffield Wednesday board had sacked David Pleat and given the manager's job to Ron Atkinson. Arsenal's visit was his first game in charge. More than 34,000 – way above Wednesday's gates at the time – turned out to see a little piece of history. Adams recognised the warning signs. Eleven months before, the Gunners had visited another club threatened by relegation, Nottingham Forest. Forest had just lost Frank Clark and handed the job to Stuart Pearce. It was Pearce's first game as boss, and Forest came from behind to beat the Gunners 2–1.

Bergkamp and Petit were still suspended. Bould had just started a ban. Vieira was still recovering. Anelka was out with an ankle injury. Wenger gave a Premiership debut to Alberto Mendez, with Overmars playing behind lone striker Wright. Arsenal played three at the back again: Adams, Grimandi and Martin Keown. The Gunners dominated the first forty minutes, without creating much beyond Stephen Hughes's flashing header. Then, three minutes before the interval, Grimandi's weak back-pass let in Andy Booth to put Wednesday ahead. Arsenal pressed forward, without seriously threatening Kevin Pressman. Parlour had already limped off after a lunge by Peter Atherton. Grimandi departed with his left arm in a sling. Four minutes from time, Guy Whittingham touched in Benito Carbone's cross and the Owls fans celebrated Big Ron's return. United, meanwhile, had won 5–2 at Wimbledon, widening the gap to four points again.

'The result didn't reflect the play,' said Wenger. 'For most of the first half, I believed we would take at least a point. With all our injuries and suspensions, it was vital that we didn't concede a goal. Then we handed one to Wednesday.' Said Adams: 'It was a very disappointing result. We were well aware that Ron Atkinson would lift Wednesday and they'd come flying at us. But we weren't getting the ball into the box and creating chances like we were earlier in the season.'

Another anxious month lay ahead . . .

DEFEAT AND REVIVAL

Dennis Bergkamp was back for the match against Liverpool, along with Manu Petit. But Patrick Vieira and Ray Parlour were still injured. Arsène Wenger reverted to 4–4–2 with David Platt and Stephen Hughes filling the absences in midfield. Liverpool manager Roy Evans was also under pressure after Barnsley won 1–0 at Anfield the previous weekend. Paul Ince and Robbie Fowler were suspended. 'In the circumstances, I think Liverpool would settle for a draw,' said Sky analyst Andy Gray.

But they did better than that. Bergkamp and Petit were both searching for their touch again after bans and the Gunners created few chances. Liverpool strung five across midfield, with Steve McManaman breaking to support the darting Michael Owen. Ten minutes into the second half, McManaman raced on to Stig-Inge Bjornebye's throw and planted a looping shot beyond David Seaman for the only goal of the game. It was Arsenal's first home defeat. The Gunners had rarely looked like equalising. Injuries and suspensions had taken their toll, and the lack of creativity bothered Wenger again.

Now Arsenal were seven points behind Manchester United in the title race. Record-breaker Ian Wright was going through a goal drought; Nicolas Anelka was injured. Critics who'd welcomed Wenger's fresh approach started asking questions, particularly about the sale of John Hartson and Paul Merson. As Nigel Clarke wrote in the *Daily Mail*: 'Arsène Wenger seemed to be the master manager. But until he wins something, judgement will be reserved on the Frenchman who looks as if he belongs behind the desk of the local library. Wright has suddenly hit the wall. So where was the cover for him when he stopped scoring? Wenger should have recognised that when selling off the family treasures like Merson and Hartson.'

Wenger and the players addressed the situation at a team meeting. Wenger spoke first, then Tony Adams initiated a lively debate. As one senior player said afterwards: 'A few cages got rattled.' It

---

Marc Overmars lobs Tim Flowers for Arsenal's goal against Blackburn.

JVC

wasn't a case of scoring points at the expense of colleagues; more like players expressing their own professional pride and hunger to succeed.

That Saturday, at Newcastle, Wright scored his first goal for nine weeks, heading home Bergkamp's centre to beat the Geordies 1–0. Arsenal defended resolutely for the last half hour as Newcastle, still without the injured Alan Shearer, piled on the pressure. 'We defended with great collective solidity,' said Wenger. The energetic Parlour's return gave the Gunners another lift. And Wright was buzzing. Said Wenger: 'When a forward is not scoring, it's vital that he maintains his contribution to the team. Ian did that and was rewarded with a goal.'

Adams was delighted. 'We sorted things out among ourselves after the Liverpool game,' he said afterwards. 'The result was the win at Newcastle, which I thought was our best away display of the season. Our success wasn't just down to individuals. It was an all-round team performance, maybe the first time that everyone has knitted together solidly. We had shape, organisation and commitment – qualities which bring you points even when you're not at your best.'

Optimism reigned as Blackburn came to Highbury on 13 December. But it didn't last beyond the sixty-fifth minute, when Rovers

Emmanuel Petit with two young fans at the Junior Gunners Christmas party.

Dennis Bergkamp sets up Ian Wright's winner at Newcastle.

went 2–1 up. Marc Overmars, outrunning Rovers' offside trap, had lobbed Tim Flowers to give Arsenal an eighteenth-minute lead. Jason Wilcox had driven Blackburn level after a catalogue of Arsenal errors. Then Kevin Gallacher controlled Chris Sutton's flick, outpaced Adams and shot over Seaman to make it 2–1. Tim Sherwood hit the bar, then scored Blackburn's third. Only Martin Keown's pace and recovery tackles saved Arsenal from a worse defeat.

Adams, outstanding at Newcastle the previous week, looked surprisingly sluggish. Owen's nippiness in the Liverpool game had suggested problems. Injuries had taken their toll on the Gunners' skipper too. Soon, he would fly to the south of France for rehabilitation, and triumphantly resurrect his season. That was weeks away, though, and Arsenal were now thirteen points behind United. As Ken Jones wrote in the *Independent* the following Monday: 'You wouldn't bet on Wenger's team with someone else's money.'

Wright, criticised by a section of fans in the matches against Sheffield Wednesday and Liverpool, got into an argument with supporters who were shouting at the dressing room from Avenell Road. That incident was smoothed over. But there more problems ahead. Suddenly, there was supposed to be a split between the English players in the camp and Wenger's French imports. In the *Mirror*, Mike Walters wrote: 'Although the cliques are based on an Anglo-French split, the language barrier itself is not at the root of the problem. But some of the old guard assembled under George Graham are concerned that, on the pitch, Gallic subtlety is in danger of marginalising English grit.'

Petit answered that. 'I can speak for all the French players at Arsenal when I say that we feel as though we have to work that much harder to demonstrate that we're here on merit. We have had to cope with press suggestions that the French players lack the will to win or a competitive instinct. That's just not true. When we lose or don't play to our potential, that hurts very deeply. Arsène Wenger treats us exactly the same as the rest of the squad. In training, he addresses us in English. There are no special translations in French. His attitude is that it's up to us to learn the language and adapt. We have Duncan [Duncan Bennetts, an interpreter provided by the club] as our English teacher. Apart from that, there are no allowances.'

Wenger was philosophical. 'It's natural that the French players will talk together,' he said. 'To suggest the English and the French players don't get on together is not true. To suggest the French players don't battle either is just not right. How can you say that about players like Patrick and Manu, and the others? They have been surprised at some of the comments. I told them that, as foreign players, they will be the first to be accused if things go wrong. But I can say that they have all been accepted by the players and fans. The spirit here is good.'

Critical eyes were trained on the Gunners when they met Wimbledon at Selhurst Park on 22 December. The first half was goalless; then the floodlights failed. Referee Dermot Gallagher consulted Wenger and Dons manager Joe Kinnear. Said Wenger: 'We agreed that if the lights came back on by 9.35 p.m. we would go out and play. But when the lights went out the second time, it was the right decision to abandon the game. Otherwise we could have been waiting until midnight.'

The consensus outside Highbury was that the lights had gone out on Arsenal's title chances too; but the players didn't think so. They'd been talking again, after the defeat by Blackburn. Wenger later reflected on the significance of that meeting: 'It was the turning point of the season.' Senior players – like Adams – stressed that if Arsenal could put a run together like their twelve-game unbeaten start, they could yet challenge United. Vieira was available again. So was Anelka. Vieira and Petit – roles slightly changed to protect the back four – would develop into an inspired combination, in defence and attack; and Anelka would blossom. As Parlour said: 'United are in the driving seat. But we can still catch them if we perform like we did earlier in the season. Everyone is back fit now, so I expect we'll start climbing the table.'

The pre-Christmas festivities had brought the players closer together too. On

Marc Overmars, Ray Parlour and Dennis Bergkamp visit the children's ward at the Whittington hospital.

16 December the whole squad, watched by Sky Sports' cameras, had attended the now-famous Junior Gunners' Christmas party. Then they divided into three groups to visit the children's wards of local hospitals: the Whittington at Highgate, Queen Elizabeth's in Hackney, and the Middlesex. The players' own Christmas party had cemented bonds as well. 'We could relax in private and have a bit of a laugh together,' said Adams.

Before he went to France, Adams had commented: 'Injuries and suspensions have disrupted our pattern. But everything Arsenal have won, we've won collectively. That's how we must approach the rest of the season.' And at the end of the season, Hughes, though never sure of a place himself, summed up: 'I think everyone has got into the Highbury spirit. As players, we became very close, which is why we played so well together.'

Wenger had sensed the Christmas vibes too. 'There is a strong mentality in the team,' he said. 'I believe we will show it on the pitch . . .'

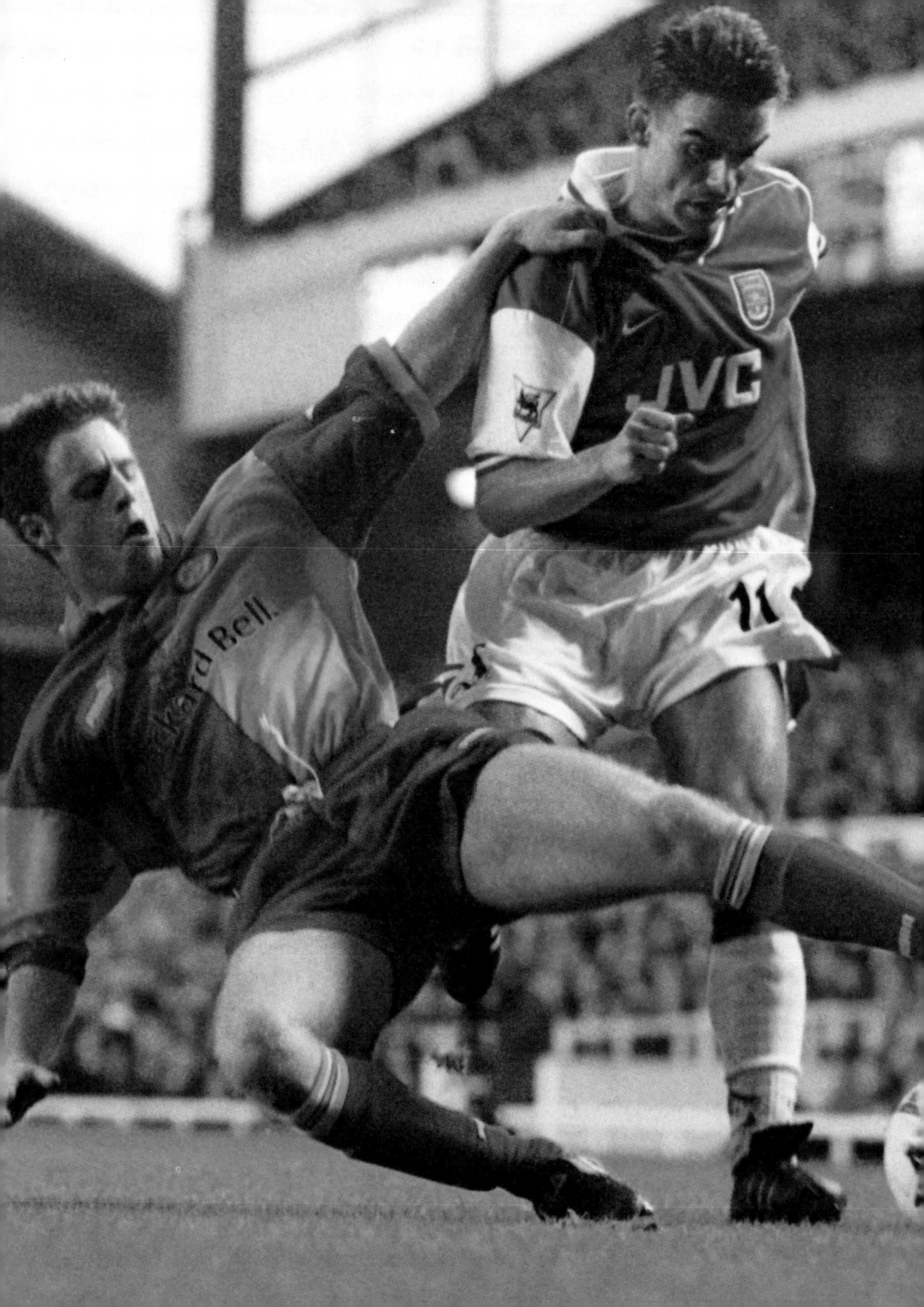
JVC

OVERMARS

The date was 10 January 1998. Leeds, on the rise under George Graham, were the visitors to Highbury. While the media tried to build up the contest between Arsène Wenger and Graham, Wenger was keen to play it down. 'I realise there will be comparisons because George is back at Highbury. But he has been back twice before, so it's not a new situation,' said Wenger.

The second of those visits had been in the FA Cup fourth round, eleven months earlier. Leeds had defended for most of the night, broke out for Rod Wallace to score, then clung on for a 1–0 win. Typical Graham, and the prospect was raised again. Graham himself added fuel to the flames by making uncomplimentary comments about Arsenal's directors.

The vibes from Elland Road were confident. Graham and his assistant, Arsenal appearance record-holder David O'Leary, knew all about the pressures on the Gunners. In the end though, they went home pointless – thanks to a titanic second-half performance by Marc Overmars. Overmars's two blistering goals marked a turning point for the Gunners – and for the Dutch winger.

Recalled O'Leary: 'When we went to Highbury, Arsenal had some problems behind the scenes. Results weren't going that well, and it didn't seem the happiest club. Without going into detail, it was obvious things weren't quite right, and the atmosphere afterwards was a bit strange. Since then, things really got sorted. The spirit appears wonderful, and Arsenal have played beautiful football. I think that game was a watershed for them. We were going well, but they won 2–1 with two great strikes by Overmars, who'd had a very quiet first half. After that, Arsenal's season really took off.'

So did Overmars. Wenger's biggest summer signing had not found it easy to settle into English football. Despite goals at Southampton and Everton, plus two in the Highbury rout of West Ham, he had been substituted in eight of Arsenal's first ten

---

Marc Overmars takes on Leeds right back Alan Maybury.

Ray Parlour, Dennis Bergkamp and Lee Dixon lead the congratulations for Overmars's first goal against Leeds.

league games. Overmars knew what to expect when he arrived. 'In Holland, the pace of the game changes from fast to slow. In England the pace is very high for ninety minutes. That's something I have to get used to,' he said.

As Arsenal struggled through November and December though, questions were raised about the Dutch winger, as well as Arsenal's Frenchmen. Could Overmars last the pace in the English game? How fit was he? Had the severe knee injury that kept him out of Euro 96 taken the edge off his game? Overmars was about to answer those doubts, triumphantly. He'd given a clue four days earlier, in the Coca-Cola Cup quarter-final at rain-drenched Upton Park. Wenger thought West Ham did well to get the game on. The pitch was sodden. That didn't worry Overmars – especially in the second half, when he repeatedly pulled inside, making runs from deep that caused West Ham all sorts of problems. At the end of one such run, he poached the goal that ensured a 2–1 win.

'Arsène Wenger had changed the system slightly and I enjoyed the change,' explained Overmars. 'I could come in off the wing and make runs into the middle. That gave me more chance to link up with the strikers and have more shots at goal.'

At half time in the Leeds game, however, the visitors were surprised Overmars hadn't made more of an impression. Graham had detailed young full-back Alan Maybury to mark the Dutchman. 'We couldn't believe how well he did against Overmars in the first half,' recalled Leeds goalkeeper Nigel Martyn. 'Then Overmars came to life.'

The goals were similar, both cutting in on his favourite right foot, then unleashing bullet shots from the edge of the box. Overmars put Arsenal ahead on the hour. Jimmy Floyd Hasselbaink equalised within nine minutes. Three minutes later, Overmars buried the Gunners' winner. His colleagues never had any doubts about Overmars's value. As Tony Adams said: 'He gives us something extra. When he has the ball he draws two players to him, which creates more space for everyone else.'

Said Dennis Bergkamp: 'Marc attracts defenders and gives me more space to run into. He knows where and how I like the ball and that's another big help.' Now the fans appreciated the ex-Ajax star too.

Afterwards, Graham revealed how he'd long admired Overmars, saying he wanted to bring the Dutchman to Highbury in 1994. But Overmars had already commented: 'At the time, I had just signed a new contract for Ajax and the team looked like doing good things [they won the Champions League that season]. At the same time, I got the feeling that Arsenal weren't reaching the standards they should have been. Things are different now though.'

Different for Overmars too, who quickly added goals at Middlesbrough in the FA Cup, and scored the first against Chelsea in the first leg of the Coca-Cola Cup semi-final. 'My finishing hasn't always been my strongest point. But now I feel confident about it, and I want to score some more,' said Overmars.

Ask Manchester United – or Newcastle, after the FA Cup final! Overmars chipped in with the second in the 5–0 demolition of Wimbledon that sent the Gunners to the top of the table with games in hand. The next weekend, he scored the vital second that killed off Barnsley at Oakwell, bursting inside again to finish David Platt's pass after a host of chances had gone begging.

It was Overmars's winning tackle that fed Manu Petit for the decisive goal against Derby, which set up the carnival finale against Everton. Overmars turned Everton inside out, twisting inside and outside. It was notable that he struck both his goals with his left foot, both after thrilling dribbles at speed. That lifted his total for the season to fifteen – his best ever. 'My best before was thirteen for Ajax, so I was delighted to beat that. But I wasn't thinking about records when I scored against Everton,' he said. 'My first goal put us two up and gave Everton no chance to come back. When I scored the third, I felt we could relax as a team, because we had the Championship within our grasp.' At Wembley, he made it sixteen, leaving Alessandro Pistone trailing, before beating Shay Given.

At the end of last season, Arsène Wenger diagnosed that Arsenal needed more pace and penetration from the flanks. Overmars has supplied both with a vengeance. His temperament has been a bonus. Never booked – despite the whackings he's taken – Overmars has also settled calmly into life in London – a similar city to Amsterdam, only much bigger.

'Marc has been very important,' said Wenger, who was prepared to sign the Dutchman while other clubs wondered about the extent of his knee injury. 'Highbury is a narrow pitch. So we needed pace on the wing. Marc has given us that. So has Ray Parlour on the right. It wasn't easy for Marc at the start. It takes time to adapt to English football. That's why he seemed to tire towards the end of our early matches. He also had to adjust from being an out-and-out winger to a wide player in a 4–4–2 formation. But he has a very positive attitude and I always believed he would succeed. After what he achieved for Ajax, I never had any doubts that he could perform throughout an English season. He always performed on the big occasion too, as he showed at Manchester United and at Wembley. I don't think any other wide player could have scored that number of goals. He has been such a big player for us – not just for his goals, but also because of the chances he has created for others. He has made a crucial contribution to our success.'

Said Pat Rice: 'He seems to get better as each game goes on. He has such a high energy level.'

Brian Marwood, left winger for Graham's 1989 champions, added: 'His form since Christmas has been exceptional. He has tremendous pace, quick feet, and he's always likely to score.'

And when Overmars reflects on the Gunners' brilliant season, he may think of that second half against Leeds with fond memories.

Marc Overmars scores the first goal at Wembley.

JVC
AGFA

ADAMS

He started the season trying to assert his fitness. He ended it lifting the Championship and the FA Cup. In between he overcame a career-threatening crisis and returned to lead the Gunners to glory. 'He', of course, is Tony Adams, the most successful captain in Arsenal's history. Since he took over from Kenny Sansom in March 1988, Adams has wrapped his hands around more silverware than any Gunners skipper; more even than other legendary captains like Tom Parker, Joe Mercer and Frank McLintock; winning the Championship three times, the FA Cup twice, the Coca-Cola Cup and the Cup-Winners' Cup.

But Adams has done more than lift trophies. He has overcome his problems in the full glare of the public spotlight. In 1996, he told the world he was an alcoholic. He was also coming to terms with a marriage break-up; and he played most of the 1996–97 season troubled by a persistent ankle injury. Because of that injury, Adams had seven weeks of pre-season training instead of other players' five. 'That gave me the chance to take things nice and gradually,' he said. The only pain he felt in the pre-season games was a whack in the ribs from an opponent at Sittingbourne.

Adams was suspended for the Gunners' first two matches of the 1997–98 season, a leftover from 1996–97. After reserve outings against Portsmouth and Southampton, he returned for the UEFA Cup tie in Salonika. Two weeks later, Adams was saying: 'I feel fine and I'm relishing each match. After two years of problems with knees, ankles and ribs, I'm just happy to be playing again. I remember coming off in big games against Manchester United and Newcastle last season. There were other times when it was touch and go whether I even started. Now I'm pain-free and it's my responsibility to motivate others.'

The UEFA Cup defeat by PAOK apart, Adams's recovery looked complete. He was a rock for England in Rome when Glenn Hoddle's team drew 0–0 to qualify for France

---

Tony Adams and Crystal Palace's Bruce Dyer battle for the ball in the FA Cup fifth round replay.

TDK
6

'98. Arsenal were mounting an early-season title challenge. Then the problems started piling up. The Gunners went down 0–3 at Derby on 1 November after what Adams called 'some very un-Arsenal type defending'.

The following Sunday, David Platt's header saw off Manchester United 3–2 at Highbury. Adams's ankle was inflamed after the game: cue the speculation. 'I read about possible operations, being out for six weeks, and so on. Well, the last thing I want at this stage of my career – at thirty-one – is more major surgery,' said Adams. He went to see a surgeon for a check-up, had an injection to reduce the inflammation, then rested. He joined the England squad for the friendly against Cameroon though he didn't train or play. Arsène Wenger rested him for the Coca-Cola Cup tie against Coventry.

Tony Adams.

Adams returned for the defeats at Sheffield Wednesday and at home to Liverpool, but something was wrong. He wasn't playing at full power. That worried him. He feared falling below his own standards. He was concerned that more surgery might affect him for the rest of his life, far beyond his football career. 'I wasn't doing myself justice,' he said. 'I had doubts about my ankle which affected my form. Some days I got out of bed and couldn't walk properly. It took me a long time to get going in the mornings. Training became a strain. I wasn't happy, having treatment and controlling things with tablets. I even wondered to myself if it was all over.'

When Arsenal won 1–0 at Newcastle on 6 December, Adams looked more like his old self. That illusion was shattered when Blackburn won 3–1 at Highbury the following week. *Match of the Day*'s pundits were quick to pinpoint Adams's lack of mobility as Kevin

Gallacher and Chris Sutton shredded the Gunners. 'It wasn't the Arsenal we'd known and played against so often,' said Gallacher. 'And Tony Adams seemed to be struggling.'

'I couldn't carry on like that. I was letting myself down,' said Adams. 'Looking back, that game was a turning point, a big motivational force. I made mistakes that cost us goals. I remember how upset the fans were. I looked on the Internet afterwards and read the comments, some about me. I react to criticism, I always have done. I always want to prove critics wrong, and I had to do something. I'd been carrying injuries for two years and I knew there were question marks against me. My pride wouldn't let me be an also-ran and just get by.'

By now, Adams was also nursing a back injury which put more pressure on his joints and body. But Wenger was understanding and came up with a constructive solution. Adams had received treatment in France before. Now he went to the Cote d'Azur for intensive therapy, up to seven hours a day. At home the rumours soon started. Tony was back on the booze. Tony had been sent home from London Colney. As Ian Ridley, who helped Tony write his own book (due out this autumn), said: 'Total nonsense. He'd touched nothing stronger than Earl Grey tea.'

Within a few weeks, Adams would nail those rumours. While England was shivering in January, he was running on the beach in the south of France. 'Tony benefited from a detailed exercise programme and individual attention,' said Wenger. 'Psychologically, it was also good for him to have a change from our usual routine.' 'It was make-or-break time,' said Adams. His specialist conditioning coach, Tiberce Darrou, drove him through a gruelling schedule. Darrou, known for his work with tennis players and the Paris St-Germain squad, stretched Adams's ankle to the limit, testing and probing to see if it would stand the strain. 'The first two days were so tough. But I stayed the journey,' said Adams.

The breakthrough came after Adams had trained with the Antibes basketball team. 'Can you feel some explosive power now?' asked Darrou.

Adams nodded. 'I feel ready to blow up!' he replied.

That gave him the confidence in his body that he needed. 'What I did in France was ten times harder than playing a football match,' he said. 'Then I wanted to show everyone that I was one hundred per cent again.'

Adams returned to England on 9 January. He made his comeback in a reserve game against Chelsea at Enfield eleven days later. Then he led the Gunners in the Coca-Cola Cup semi-final against Chelsea on 28 January. After that, Adams missed just two games, both through suspension, as the Gunners charged on to clinch the Championship against Everton and win the FA Cup final.

At Wembley in 1993, Arsenal had needed Andy Linighan's last-minute extra-time header to beat Sheffield Wednesday in a replay. This time, Nicolas Anelka's goal – that made it 2–0 – killed the final with twenty minutes left. There was another difference too. Wenger's dietary and physiological regimes had created a new climate at Highbury, mineral water had become the 'in' drink. Old players smiled when they remembered past glory nights. But Adams had made up his own mind. When he needed support, he sought it from his alcohol counsellor, Steve Jacobs. 'Alcohol wiped out parts of my life. Now we've won the Double and I can enjoy it clear-headed,' said Adams.

'Tony has been a huge influence in the second half of the season,' said Wenger. 'We have seen the real Tony Adams since January.' Adams scored three important goals on that Championship run-in; against Southampton, Wimbledon, and – the pick of the bunch – that left-foot scorcher from Steve Bould's delicate through ball to make it 4–0 against Everton.

Terry Burton, who's done so much for Wimbledon over the last decade, was youth team coach when Adams first arrived at Highbury, having been spotted as a gangly thirteen-year-old by Arsenal's now chief scout, Steve Rowley. 'He looked special from the start,' said Burton. 'He was a tenacious defender, strong in the air and he read the game from a very early age. He never knew when he was beaten either. How important that has been in Tony's career.' 'He was a great organiser with such a mature presence on the pitch,' recalled Don Howe. 'He's always had those leadership qualities. And he's always reacted to criticism. Tony's problems have been well publicised, but there's never been a time when he's gone and hidden.'

Neither man was surprised by that goal against Everton. 'He's always been dangerous going forward,' said Burton. 'Not just at free kicks and corners either. He's always been a more skilful player than some people have realised. I'll never forget a goal he scored against West Ham in the South East Counties League, when he played a one-two on the halfway line, another one-two on the edge of the box, then "passed" the ball into their net.' Wenger has given Adams freedom to play like that again. 'He lets us go out and do the job, and we've responded. At times I think we're flying!' said Adams.

The Arsenal captain has found his own voice too. It was Adams who initiated the debate that led to the tactical changes which transformed Arsenal's season. It's Adams, along with PFA rep Martin Keown, who represents the players' views to the directors. Adams, following Wenger's example, set the tone for the Gunners' 'one game at a time' end to the season. Adams was a leading mover in the Gunners' decision to donate their FA Cup final pool money to the Arsenal Charitable Trust.

Once, he admitted, he always tried to leave games behind Ian Wright, because the waiting press men would automatically swarm around Wrighty and leave Adams free to go home. Now he handles these occasions on his own terms. He knows who he can rely on. After the FA Cup semi-final, Adams was one of the last out of the Arsenal dressing room. 'Sorry, guys,' he said to the waiting tabloid reporters, 'I can't speak to you now. Our bus is about to go, and I've got to get on.' Then, spotting a friendly face at the exit door, he whispered: 'Give me a call on the mobile tomorrow.'

Adams's attitude is hardly surprising, given the *Daily Mirror*'s disgraceful 'donkey' slur (the man responsible was allegedly an Arsenal fan) when he was leading the Gunners to George Graham's first Championship nine years ago. Or the reaction to Adams's 1990–91 prison sentence for drink-driving; not so much justice as a Christmas deterrent to less famous motorists. But he's also discovered an impressive fluency at press conferences, when he thinks it's right. This is not the Adams of memory. Adams the old skipper would thump his fist and shout. Now he leads by example just the same, but keeps overt gestures to a minimum. 'I don't feel the need for them any more.'

A few years ago, a perceptive critic wrote of Adams: 'When he pulls on a football shirt, he's like Clark Kent changing into Superman. The football pitch or the training ground is where he feels comfortable.' Not now. The Arsenal captain has moved from his old south Essex haunts to south-west London, and he's rediscovered life outside football. He's a doting father; he spends hours of his leisure time with his head buried in books; he plays the piano for relaxation (though he'll never play in public); he's become a keen gardener. And he can chuckle at himself. At the height of the Championship race when matches came thick and fast, Adams laughed: 'All these games are doing nothing for my garden.' Then he went out and led Arsenal to the Double.

As Bob Wilson said: 'The fans know that Tony is committed to the Arsenal – and they admire him for the way he's overcome his problems.'

Once Adams symbolised the 'old' Gunners. Now he's at the heart of 'new Arsenal'.

Tony Adams heads the first goal in the 5-0 win over Wimbledon that took Arsenal to the top of the league.

JVC
10

ARSENAL FIGHT BACK

Arsenal's fight-back began in unlikely circumstances with a 2–1 win over Leicester at Highbury on Boxing Day. David Platt headed the Gunners into a thirty-sixth minute lead. Then Leicester captain Steve Walsh, sensing the approach of his old foe Ian Wright, scored one of the most bizarre own goals of the season. Wright and Marc Overmars, the two Arsenal attackers furthest forward, could hardly believe it as Walsh lobbed his own keeper Kasey Keller from nearly forty yards.

Neil Lennon pulled one back after a mix-up between David Seaman and Steve Bould. It was not an impressive performance. Arsène Wenger was frank: 'We were terrible in the last ten minutes. We couldn't keep the ball or pass it and that made me nervous.' But Arsenal were glad of three points after their recent problems. 'It was crucial for us to win,' said Wenger. 'That will help us in the future – and maybe now we can get back to our normal game.'

Dennis Bergkamp scores the first goal against Southampton at Highbury.

The derby at Tottenham soon followed. Spurs were pumped up with Klinsmania following the return of the German striker, on loan from Sampdoria. White Hart Lane was being re-built and Arsenal received only 855 tickets, so the game was beamed back to an audience of over 8000 at Highbury. With Wright suspended, Dennis Bergkamp played despite illness. 'In different circumstances, he wouldn't have played, but we needed him,' admitted Arsène Wenger. Bergkamp wasn't himself, but still set up a glorious chance – with a delicate back-heel – for Nicolas Anelka after Allan Nielsen's early goal. Anelka had Ian Walker beaten, but his shot cannoned off a post. Ray Parlour cut inside to hit the equaliser, a powerful shot that deflected off Ramon Vega.

Wenger was surprised that Spurs played so much in the air towards Klinsmann, one of his Monaco 'old boys'. But that suited Arsenal. In the absence of Tony Adams, off for rehabilitation in the south of France, Steve Bould and Martin Keown were outstanding in the second half. It was a sign of things to come. Meanwhile, Manchester United were offering their pursuers a little hope by going down 2–3 to Coventry after two goals in the last four minutes – a Dion Dublin penalty and Darren Huckerby's low shot. That was another sign of things to come.

Cup ties occupied the Gunners' next two matches: a disappointing home FA Cup draw against Port Vale, followed by an impressive Coca-Cola Cup quarter-final win at West Ham. The following league game, against Leeds, was crucial to Arsenal's revival and to Overmars's emergence as a Highbury hero. That 2–1 win deserves a section to itself – and gets it. For Wenger, victory brought blessed relief. A lot of critics had their barbs already thought out, had Arsenal lost to George Graham's rejuvenated team.

After a penalty shoot-out replay win at Port Vale, marred by the loss of Wright, the Gunners visited another side with a new lease of life: Gordon Strachan's Coventry. Noel Whelan struck for the Sky Blues after twenty-one minutes and the home side piled on the pressure. But Bergkamp put Arsenal back in contention five minutes after half time when he lobbed Magnus Hedman to level the scores. Seven minutes later, Anelka bundled home Arsenal's second. Once upon a time Coventry would have folded, but not now. Dublin equalised from a penalty in the sixty-seventh minute awarded against Patrick Vieira for handball.

Seaman broke a finger making an important save. Vieira was sent off after protesting too loudly to referee Stephen Lodge about the penalty. Coventry had Paul Williams red-carded too, after felling Bergkamp on the edge of the box. Television replays suggested there was little contact, though enough to knock Bergkamp off balance. Coventry's ex-Feyenoord midfielder George Boateng asked Bergkamp in Dutch how strong the challenge was. Referee Lodge later came under pressure to annul the dismissal, but refused. The 'Bergkamp dives' lobby were in their element, though wrong.

'Are they being serious?' said an obviously angry Bergkamp. 'If I am through on the goalkeeper I don't ever fall over on purpose, because I always back myself to beat him and score. What happened when I intercepted Williams's back-header earlier? I ran on and put the ball in the net for our first goal. I am not a cheat. My conscience is clear.' Amid the fuss, Matthew Upson's composed Premiership debut almost passed unnoticed.

Two crucial points in the title race had been lost by Arsenal. Or had they? On Monday night, Kevin Davies poached the only goal as Southampton, Manchester United's bogey side at The Dell, beat the champions 1–0. Maybe United's obsession with the Champions League was already playing on their players' minds. But at the time, it seemed only a minor hiccup because Alex Ferguson's men held such a strong lead.

By the time Dave Jones's much-improved Saints came to Highbury on 31 January, the Gunners had disposed of Middlesbrough in the FA Cup fourth round and taken a 2–1 lead (it should have been more) against Chelsea in the Coca-Cola Cup semi-final. Adams was back to fitness.

Nicolas Anelka makes it 3-0 against Saints.

Lee Dixon commented before the match: 'As far as the Championship goes, you're allowed one loss of form during the season. We've had that, and can't afford another.' Dixon, a Manchester City fan as a boy, spoke some prophetic words too. He'd seen Ferguson on television the previous week, discussing United's possible challengers. Ferguson hadn't mentioned Arsenal. 'He didn't include us among the teams he saw as a threat and we'll be looking to show that was a mistake,' said Dixon. 'If we can repeat the unbeaten run we put together at the start of the season, then we'll be in a position to make Mr Ferguson think again.'

Southampton came to defend. But once Bergkamp had made the breakthrough, seventeen minutes after half time, Arsenal were rampant. Adams headed the second. 'It was long overdue,' he said. 'I scored because I was fit and free in my movement again.' Bergkamp created the third for Anelka. Alex Manninger kept his first Premiership clean sheet. As Adams said, 'Once we'd gone ahead, they couldn't change their approach to come back at us. We killed the game pretty fast after that.'

Meanwhile, United were suffering another shock defeat, 0–1 at home to Leicester who had been erratic for the last month. Tony Cottee, recently returned from

Malaysia, pinched the only goal. And by the time Stephen Hughes's two early goals had seen off Chelsea in a physical contest, the Gunners were only six points behind United with a game in hand: United had dropped a point at home to Bolton the day before. Said Wenger: 'Stephen hit an excellent shot for our first goal, and he was brave with his header for our second.' But there was a price to be paid. Referee Dermot Gallagher booked Bergkamp in the last minute: another card towards another suspension. 'I wish he'd blown the final whistle thirty seconds earlier,' lamented Wenger.

Injuries and suspensions were taking their toll. Wright had come on as a sub against Chelsea, but wouldn't start another league game until May. Adams was suspended. Keown – out with a head wound – and Seaman were still searching for fitness. Seaman was a worry, despite understudy Manninger's excellent form. 'His finger fracture is at a delicate point, between the points of the bones,' said Wenger. 'That creates pressure as the bones pull. He may need another week or two.' In the event, it was to be another month before Seaman returned.

Arsenal drew 0–0 with Palace in the FA Cup fifth round and faced another replay. The following Wednesday, they lost the second leg of the Coca-Cola Cup semi-final 1–3 at Stamford Bridge, while Manchester United won their rearranged league match at Aston Villa 2–0. The Gunners' knocks, bans and absences because of international calls were piling up as Crystal Palace's league visit approached on 21 February. That would be another crucial date in Arsenal's season . . .

Stephen Hughes heads the second goal against Chelsea in the Premiership.

THE GOLDEN OLDIES

It was the last minute of the FA Cup final, Arsenal's closing game of a gruelling season. They led 2–0. Alan Shearer had battled his way into the box and prepared to shoot. Suddenly, Nigel Winterburn appeared as if from nowhere to whisk the ball to safety. That said everything about the energy and determination of the men Tony Adams calls Arsenal's 'golden oldies' – the famous back line of Lee Dixon, Steve Bould, Adams himself and Winterburn. Dixon is thirty-four now. So is Winterburn. Bould is thirty-five; Adams is thirty-one.

It was 27 August 1988 when they played together for the first time: the opening match of George Graham's first Championship season. They all had something to prove; all showed the 'hunger and desire' that Graham loves in players. They've retained that hunger too. The Gunners hammered Wimbledon 5–1 at Plough Lane. Alan Smith, who scored a hat trick that afternoon, shared in two title wins with the famous back four. 'Every year it's the last year for Arsenal's defence. But I think there's at least another year left in them,' he said. 'They all have a great competitive spirit. They all push themselves in training, and over the years they've developed a wonderful understanding as a unit, which we may never see again at one club.'

Adams rose from the youth team. Dixon trekked around the lower divisions with Burnley, Chester and Bury before establishing himself at Stoke. In his early days at Stoke, Bould was even loaned out to Torquay, who played him at right-back. Winterburn was given a free transfer by Birmingham, then released by Oxford after a brief trial before making his name with Wimbledon. Between May 1987 and July the following year, Graham recruited first Winterburn, then Dixon and finally Bould, at a cost of little more than £1 million.

Ten years later in 1998, as the Gunners built their New Year title bid on a foundation of clean sheets – including a Premiership record of eight in a row – Graham wryly

---

Top left Lee Dixon. *Top right* Steve Bould in typical pose. *Below* Nigel Winterburn celebrates the semi-final victory over Wolves.

JVC
JVC
WALKERS
JVC

pointed out that his 'old boys' still formed the core of the side. Arsène Wenger, ever-gracious, in turn thanked Graham for leaving him such capable and determined defenders. But it was Wenger who kept the famous four together, when he might have been tempted to disband them. He likens them to good French red wine: they get even better with age. 'Their approach to the game is impeccable,' said Wenger, as he concluded new contract deals with Winterburn, Bould and Dixon in February. 'They never miss a training session and they all work very hard. I believe that what you do on the pitch is a consequence of how you conduct yourself off it and they have reaped the rewards for their professional attitude. I always wanted them to stay. They are a big part of Arsenal and the spirit of the club – and they have the quality that we need. They are super-defenders.'

Wenger stuck with that old guard when critics looked at the 'goals against' total at Christmas and concluded that the Gunners' defence had gone at last. Dixon had suffered niggling ankle trouble; Adams was about to fly to the south of France to rehabilitate his career. Remembered Winterburn: 'When things didn't go as well as hoped, people started searching for reasons and came up with explanations a mile away from reality. We'd let in more goals than expected, so it was easy to say the back four were too old, or had lost their desire. The real reason had been a general loss of form. In the games we lost at that time, we stopped defending as a team, and the back four couldn't defend against eleven.' Adams had already made that point and Wenger agreed, praising Bould and Winterburn for their consistency 'even in our bad periods'.

Once Patrick Vieira and Manu Petit took on more protective duties Arsenal's famous defensive solidity quickly returned. 'One–nil to the Arsenal' became a catch-phrase again. On 31 January, Arsenal beat Southampton 3–0 at Highbury. They didn't concede another league goal until Warren Barton hit Newcastle's consolation in the Gunners' 3–1 win on 11 April. 'We like winning games and keeping clean sheets,' said Adams.

Then there was Martin Keown. He and Adams had played centre half together for Arsenal's youth team, sixteen years earlier. Graham had brought him back to Highbury from Everton in February 1993. It was ironic that one of Graham's first acts as Arsenal's manager had been to refuse Keown a wage rise at the end of his contract in 1986. Keown moved on to Aston Villa, then to Goodison Park.

In 1989, Graham had the option of freshening up the back four with David O'Leary. In 1991, he could call on O'Leary and Andy Linighan. Now Wenger had Keown, another 'golden oldie' at thirty-two. Keown missed the first three months of the season, recovering from the shoulder injury he suffered in Le Tournoi. Then he became a pivotal figure. Keown supplied pace at the heart of the defence, first alongside Bould while Adams was in rehab, then cementing his old youth team partnership with the Arsenal captain while Bould got over a broken arm.

Keown was cup-tied when the Gunners won their Cup double in 1993. The following year he was injured and couldn't play against Parma in the Cup-Winners' Cup final. By the night of 16 May, he was celebrating the most successful season of his career, collecting Championship and FA Cup winner's medals and becoming a regular in the England squad. 'I think I felt fresh because I'd had a lay-off at the start of the season. I felt like I still had a lot of games in me,' he said.

Those 'golden oldies' will be very much part of Wenger's plans next season, whatever the manager's theories about long-term replacements. Adams will press on towards O'Leary's Arsenal appearance record. Keown will aim to build on his achievements for Arsenal and England. Bould, Winterburn and Dixon will try to extend their Highbury careers. Said Bould: 'I'm much fitter under the new regime. I wish I'd done all these stretching exercises ten years ago, because I'd have avoided some of my knocks and played more games. I may be thirty-five, but I don't think that's affected my ability to do the job. I feel as fit as ever. I want to play on for as long as I can, and there's no better place to do that than Arsenal.'

Added Winterburn: 'Every year for the last four, I've read that I was going to be replaced. You can accept that, or take it as a challenge. I've taken up the challenge and I want to be in the team again next season. Now I have the opportunity to finish my career at Arsenal. I've been here eleven years and I've always made it clear that I wanted that chance.'

Dixon is equally optimistic. 'To play for Arsenal for ten years makes me very proud. Now I'd like to make it eleven, twelve or thirteen.'

They will pass into Highbury legend: 'Uncle' Bouldy; the hunched Winterburn, the tenacious tackler with the famous left foot; and Dixon, flying up and down the right wing. But not just yet.

How long can they go on? Pat Rice has watched them closely throughout their Arsenal careers. He's in two minds: 'Until they die, or they get fed up with each other!'

Martin Keown.

PALACE

In every successful season, there's always one game that players – and fans – remember with relief. For the Gunners, that match came on 21 February 1998. Crystal Palace, later to finish bottom of the Premiership, were the visitors. Arsenal, rocked by injuries and suspensions, fielded a makeshift side. They came up with a new hero too: Gilles Grimandi.

David Seaman was recovering from a broken finger. Steve Bould was out with a broken arm. Ray Parlour was suffering from a hamstring problem. Nigel Winterburn had been hurt in the Coca-Cola Cup semi-final defeat at Chelsea three days before. Manu Petit had picked up a knock in training. Remi Garde was hurt too. Dennis Bergkamp had flu. Marc Overmars was away with Holland; Tony Adams and Chris Wreh were serving bans. Reserve defender Scott Marshall and midfielder Alberto Mendez were getting over surgery. Martin Keown started his first game for more than a month. Grimandi himself played despite a groin injury. Arsène Wenger admitted: 'If I'd had more players fit, I'd have rested him.'

As Adams said: 'I've rarely known a time when we've had so many players out with long-term injuries. It hasn't helped either that suspensions have coincided with injuries. We've only had bare numbers, just enough to fill up the team and bench.'

Arsenal were nine points behind Manchester United with two games in hand. Wenger set the game in context. 'We still have a big chance of challenging for the Championship. Whatever team we field, we must prove ourselves serious contenders.'

Alex Manninger continued to deputise for Seaman. Matthew Upson stepped in at left back for his second Premiership match. Arsenal's Premier Youth League captain, Paolo Vernazza – the Islington-born teenager who turned down Parma to join the Gunners – made his Premiership debut in midfield. Luis Boa Morte took Overmars's place on the left, with David Platt supporting Nicolas Anelka in attack. Fortunately, Palace had their own injury worries. Italian stars

Gilles Grimandi.

JVC

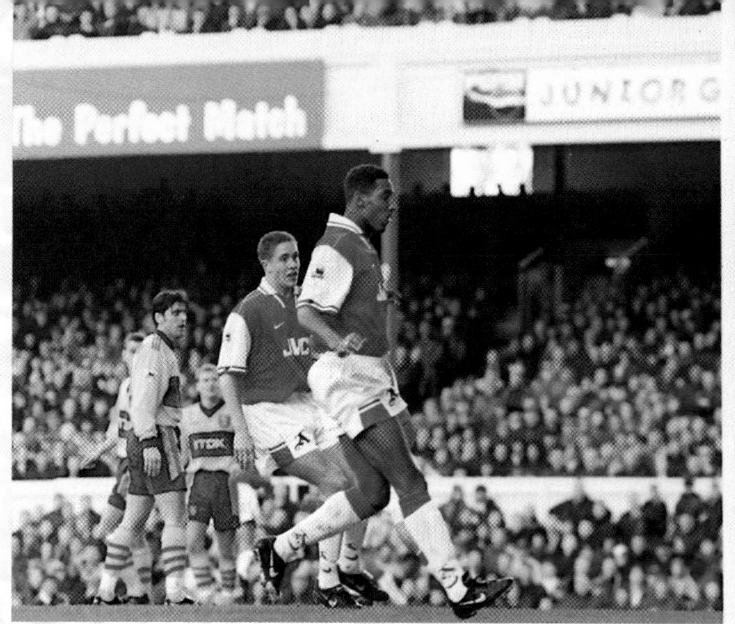

Nicolas Anelka and Matthew Upson watch the ball enter the net for Gilles Grimandi's goal.

Attilo Lombardo and Michele Padovano were sidelined. So were the Eagles' leading striker Neil Shipperley and new signing Matt Jansen. Tomas Brolin, the Swedish forward, played despite hardly any match practice. He looked clearly overweight.

It wasn't pretty to watch. With so many changes, it took Arsenal a while to settle down. Palace used centre-back Andy Roberts in midfield, in front of three more centre-backs. On the break, Palace even created the best early chance, when Bruce Dyer somehow failed to connect with Jamie Smith's centre. That roused Arsenal. Two minutes before half time, only the woodwork stopped Arsenal's youngsters from contriving their own magic moment. Vernazza swung over a corner and Upson headed against a post with Palace keeper Kevin Miller beaten.

In the second half, Patrick Vieira took command. He showed his purpose with a fifty-yard run before finding Hughes, who shot over. Grimandi proved more decisive. Vernazza measured another corner. It was only half cleared. Grimandi reacted fastest, with an instinctive volley that buried the ball beyond Miller. Highbury went wild; with relief as much as triumph.

Then Vernazza, clearly one for the future, sliced open the Palace defence with a deliciously measured through ball to Anelka, but Boa Morte miskicked with only Miller to beat. It didn't matter. Manninger pulled off a flying save from Simon Rodger's thirty-yard blast, and the Gunners were safe.

Grimandi, a summer signing from Monaco along with Manu Petit, had never been a crowd favourite. Now he was a hero. However, he paid a price. Playing for ninety minutes with that groin injury kept him out of the FA Cup replay – at Palace – the following Wednesday.

'It was very difficult for me when I first arrived,' said Grimandi. 'I made a few silly mistakes which made me feel bad and affected my confidence. But I wanted to play this game. I felt some pain which got worse as the game wore on, but I wanted to stay on for ninety minutes, because the match was so important for the Championship. I needed time to settle in at Highbury, because I'd been at Monaco for seven years. Now I feel more at home with my team-mates, though I don't usually score more than one or two goals a season. The good thing about the crowd here is that when you do well, the appreciation is very clear, and that was very encouraging for me.'

It would be hard to over-estimate the importance of Grimandi's goal to the maintenance of Arsenal's run. Said Pat Rice: 'That win was crucial to our title challenge, and Gilles' goal had a very significant look at the end of the season. The youngsters who came in did ever so well, and the performance was typical of the resilience throughout the club.'

It was good fortune that the depleted Gunners had met Palace rather than Manchester United or Liverpool. But they still had to win. David Platt summed up the players' view: 'Even with all those players missing, the way we beat Palace proved how we could cope with adversity.'

'If we win our two games in hand, we'll only be three points behind Manchester United,' said Grimandi, maybe thinking ahead to the clash at Old Trafford on 14 March.

Did he have a crystal ball, as well as a goal-scoring touch?

David Platt outruns Palace's Marc Edworthy.

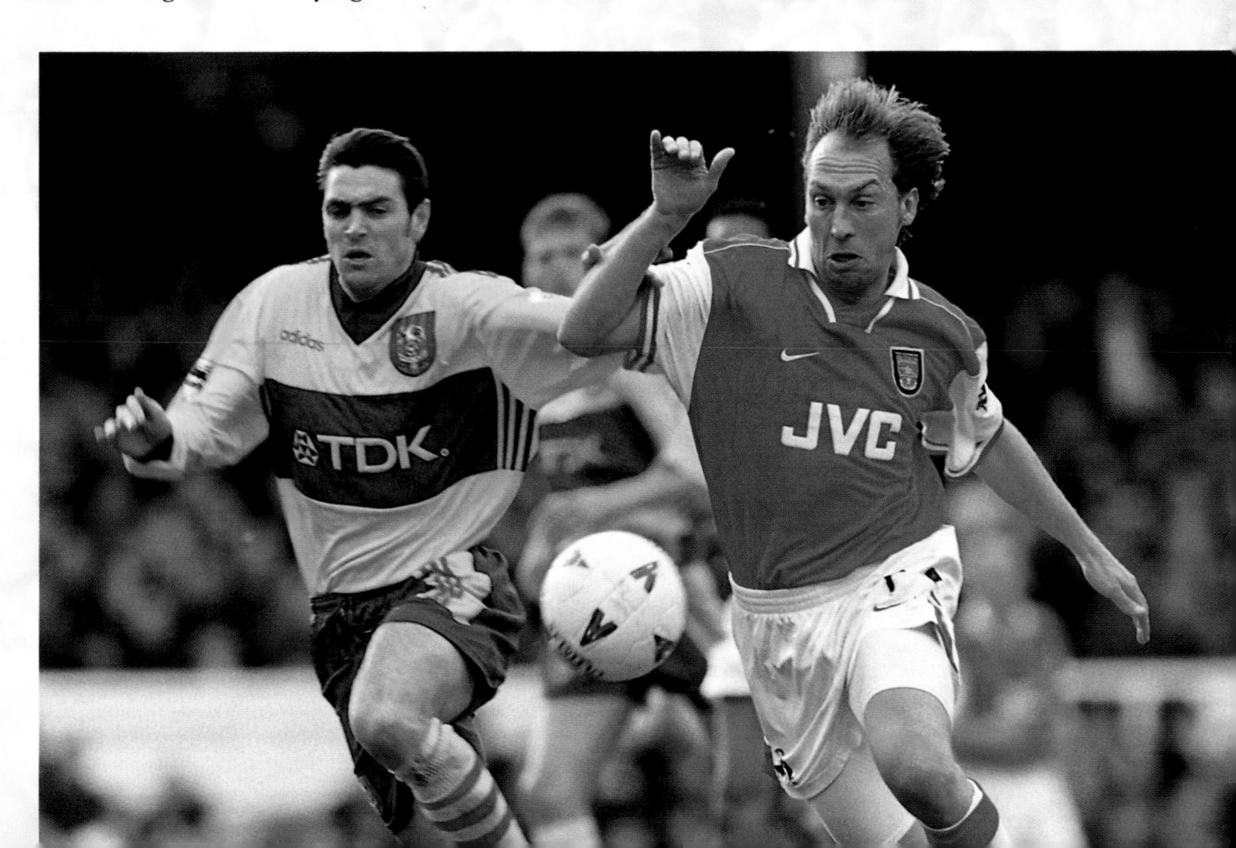

JVC
SHARP

ON TO OLD TRAFFORD

The 1–0 win over Crystal Palace left Arsenal nine points behind Manchester United, with two games in hand. While Gilles Grimandi's goal downed the Eagles, Ryan Giggs and Denis Irwin from the penalty spot, were scoring in United's 2–0 home victory over Derby. The following Saturday, Phil Neville scored the only goal of the game at Stamford Bridge – a goal that knocked Chelsea out of the title race.

Two days later, Arsenal – missing David Seaman, Steve Bould, Nigel Winterburn, Ray Parlour, Ian Wright and Dennis Bergkamp from the starting line-up – fought out a goalless draw at West Ham. Nicolas Anelka worked tirelessly as a lone striker. Martin Keown, who played the last twenty-two minutes with his head bandaged, was outstanding at the back. Sub Luis Boa Morte came closest to snatching three points with a last-minute shot. Tony Adams commented: 'A draw was a fair result. We defended well, but we didn't put enough passes together.'

Suddenly Arsenal were eleven points behind United, with three games in hand. The magazine *Match Weekly* commented: 'Arsenal's slim Premiership hopes all but disappeared in this dour game.' Said Adams: 'Realistically, United have the Championship in their grasp. But you learn never to say never until something is factually impossible. I remember in 1989, we had a massive lead over Liverpool in February; then we ended up having to beat them in the last game of the season to win the title.'

Arsène Wenger, showing the vision of an Old Testament prophet, was even more perceptive. 'I still believe Manchester United can be caught,' he said. 'They have many hard matches to play and the Champions League will be very important for them. We have a very big week ahead: Wimbledon away on Wednesday, then Manchester United at Old Trafford next Saturday.' The Gunners faced an FA Cup sixth round replay too, after drawing at home against

Patrick Vieira goes past Teddy Sheringham in the match at Old Trafford.

West Ham. United had crashed out 2–3 in a fifth round replay at Barnsley; another warning, perhaps, of disappointments ahead.

First though, Arsenal faced a rearranged game at Selhurst Park that Wednesday evening, while United travelled to West Ham. Upton Park has never been Alex Ferguson's favourite ground; not since the Hammers, then about to be relegated in bottom place, denied United the 1992 Championship by beating them 1-0. West Ham, much improved by Harry Redknapp's shrewd transfer dealings, raised themselves again. Trevor Sinclair fired them into a sixth-minute lead. United needed an equaliser in the sixty-sixth minute from Paul Scholes to earn a point.

At Selhurst, Wenger threw a new weapon into the starting line-up: the Liberian international, Chris Wreh. After twenty-one minutes, Wreh twisted on to a pass from Bergkamp and stabbed home the only goal of the match. Wimbledon piled forward in the second half, only to founder against Alex Manninger and Arsenal's famous back four. Another 'one-nil to the Arsenal'. It was ironic that the original game, on 22 December, had been abandoned because of floodlight failure at half time with the teams goalless. That was during the Gunners' dodgy period. That well-known analyst, Vinnie Jones, suggested then that Wimbledon were gaining the

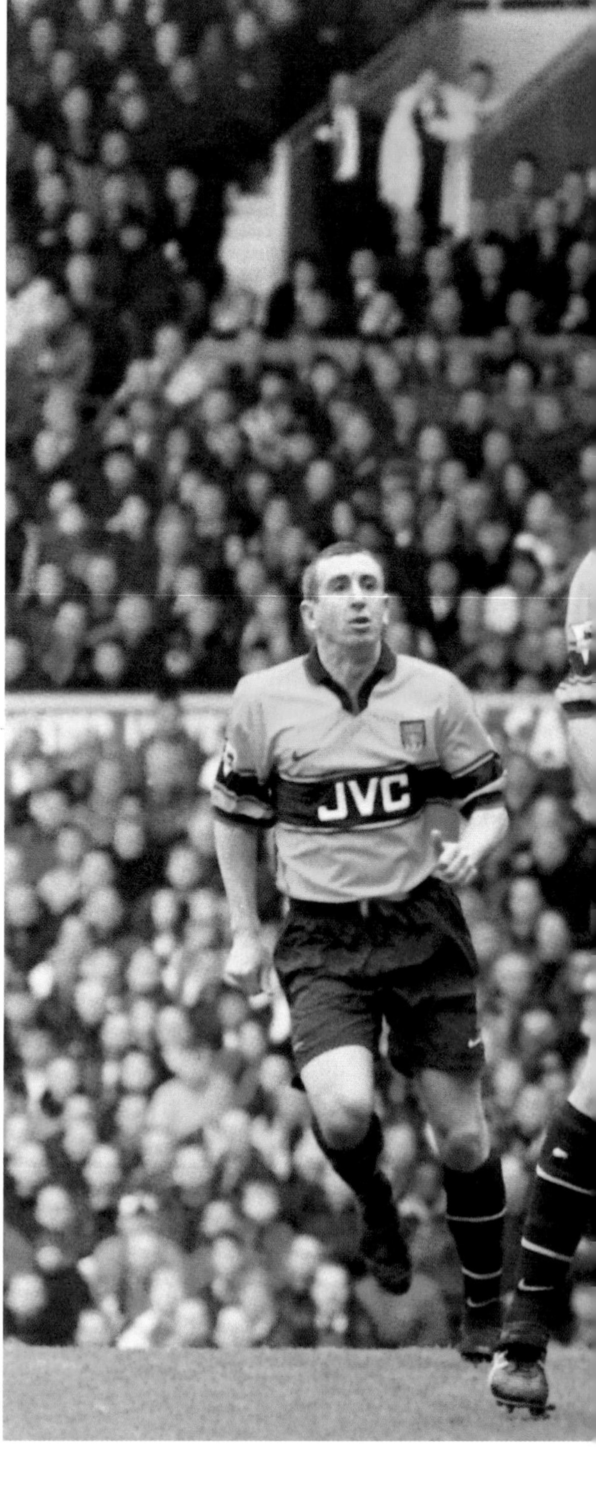

Alex Manninger saves from Manchester United's Andy Cole.

JVC

upper hand and would have won in the second half. Pure speculation, of course; but Arsenal in March bristled with a battle-hardened spirit that wasn't apparent in December. United held a nine-point lead again and the Gunners had three games in hand. 'It tees things up nicely for Old Trafford, doesn't it?' smiled Adams.

Arsenal's Double was still a figment of the imagination. United were chasing their own Double: Championship (again) and Champions League. The next fortnight would decide the destiny of their season. Maybe United's massive domination of the first half of the domestic campaign had left them thinking the title was in the bag, so they could concentrate on Ferguson's magnificent obsession, the Champions League. Only Old Trafford's closest insiders will ever really know the answer. But United were clearly missing the midfield dynamism of Roy Keane, out for the season with a knee ligament injury. They'd hit problems trying to cover knocks to Ryan Giggs and Gary Pallister too. Unlike the Gunners, United's defence had been leaking goals since Christmas.

Meanwhile, in Bould's enforced absence, Adams and Martin Keown formed a towering partnership that echoed their youth team days. And Wenger's youngsters were beginning to prove their value. Alex Manninger was a brilliant deputy for David Seaman. As Wimbledon's manager Joe Kinnear said, 'He proved to be unbeatable.' Anelka was growing into an effective replacement for Wright.

Sky's demands occasioned a morning kick-off at Old Trafford. United tried to press from the start. Manninger saved from Teddy Sheringham after Andy Cole pounced on a weak Lee Dixon back pass. 'He's pulled off some exceptional saves – and that was one of them,' said Dixon. United fans howled for a penalty when a cross hit Manu Petit's upper arm. Referee Alan Wilkie was unmoved. Arsenal's back four was also immovable. Petit and Patrick Vieira showed incredible energy ahead of them. 'Their performance was crucial,' said Wenger. 'They gave us great security to build on.'

The real drama was happening at the other end. United weren't the first or last side baffled as to how to mark Bergkamp, who dropped into the midfield space behind Wreh to deliver telling passes. Out wide, Marc Overmars's pace was destroying young defender John Curtis. Twice Overmars scythed through the United cover, only to shoot inches wide. After half an hour, Ferguson switched Gary Neville to the right to mark the Dutchman; but Overmars just kept on running. With twenty-three minutes left, Wenger pulled his master-stroke, sending on Anelka in place of the tiring Wreh. Nine minutes later, Anelka deftly nodded Bergkamp's pass into Overmars's path. This time the Dutch winger raced on and planted a deadly shot past Peter Schmeichel. 'One-nil to the Arsenal' . . . again. In the dying seconds, Schmeichel came up for a United corner and suffered a damaged hamstring which kept him out for the next three weeks.

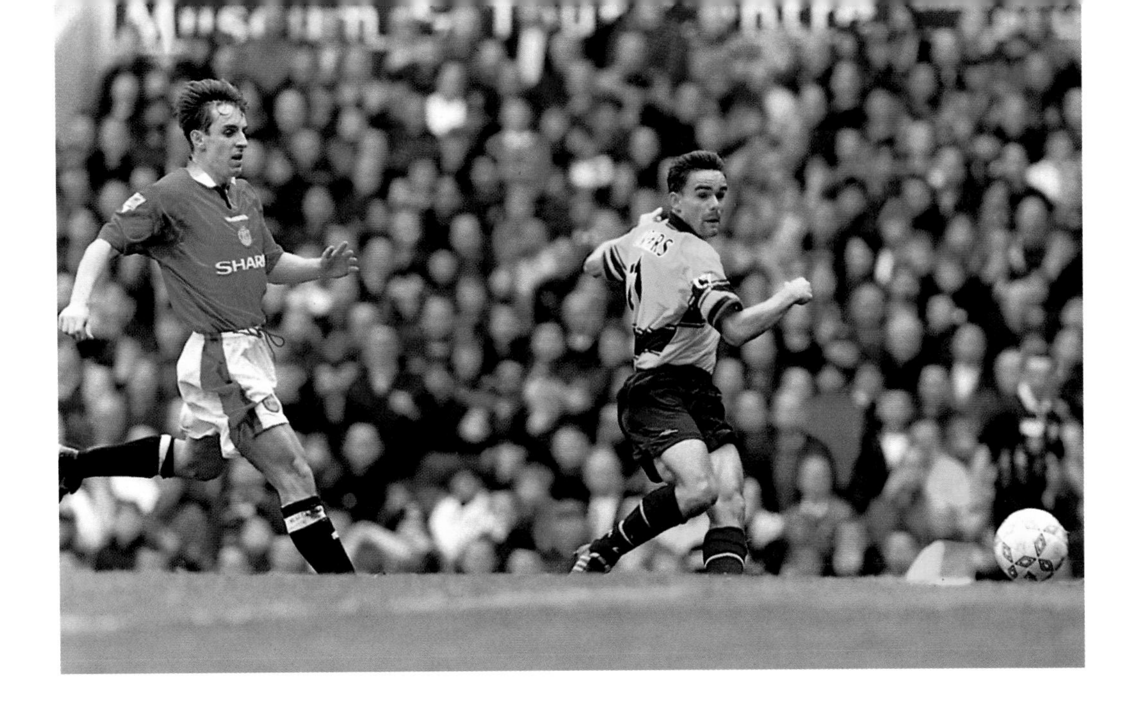

Marc Overmars scores the winner at Old Trafford.

At the end, the Arsenal players, led by Winterburn, who was savouring every second, celebrated in front of the travelling Gunners fans; while thousands in the pubs and clubs of north London went potty. 'That was our most important win of the season. I'm sure the public liked it, because it made the Championship race a genuine contest again,' smiled Wenger, with almost-English understatement.

Ferguson was already playing his mind games. United had a superior goal difference and the Old Trafford boss pointed out that Arsenal had to collect at least seven points from their games in hand to overtake United at the top. But Arsenal didn't rise to the bait. Said Adams, maybe with tongue slightly in cheek: 'Personally, I'd prefer to be in United's position, because they've got the points on the board. If we're up there with United at Easter, then we've got a chance.' Then he forecast: 'I think the next four or five league games will be crucial for both clubs.' Those words seemed blessed with insight, when Arsenal wrested top place from United on 18 April.

But, as Patrick Vieira pointed out, the real significance of that dramatic win at Old Trafford was to place the Gunners' destiny in their own hands. Said Vieira: 'At Christmas time, I thought Manchester United would almost certainly win the Championship. They were many, many points ahead, and we weren't playing at our best. Now, if we keep on winning, we will become champions.'

The following week, Arsenal's willpower dragged them through a gruelling Tuesday night FA Cup replay at West Ham. A day later, David Trezeguet's goal at Old Trafford for Wenger's old club Monaco knocked United out of the Champions League. While United's season had begun to disintegrate, Arsenal had started to prosper.

THE YOUNG ONES

'Super, super Nic, super Nic Anelka!' The words rang around Wembley. Nicolas Anelka had just buried Newcastle's hopes of a revival and ensured the FA Cup would join the Championship trophy in Highbury's silverware cabinet. In five months, the nineteen-year-old Frenchman had progressed from an untried teenager to a key figure in Arsène Wenger's plans.

Jim Smith watched one of Anelka's early appearances as a sub at Coventry in April 1997. The Derby manager, one of English football's shrewdest judges, declared: 'He looks like he's going to be a player. He has such terrific pace.'

Anelka's ability was never in doubt. At Clarefontaine, the French equivalent of the FA School of Excellence, he and Monaco's Thierry Henry were rated the finest talents of their generation. Wenger smiled with satisfaction when Arsenal finally obtained Anelka's release from Paris St Germain. Reserve coach George Armstrong called him 'one of the best eighteen-year-olds I've ever seen'. Experienced players talked of the potential he showed in training.

His challenge was to turn that potential into performance. Early signs were not promising. He was subbed on his starting debut against PAOK in Salonika, and his displays when he came into the team in November and December did little to inspire fans who still remembered Paul Merson and John Hartson. Anelka realised the problem. 'I need to become stronger on the ball and fully adapted to English football. There's a big difference in style between the game in France and England. English teams look to move from defence to attack as fast as possible. So the strikers always have to be ready to make runs because the defence and midfield are looking to pass to them early,' he said.

Anelka's goal against Manchester United in November hinted at what he might achieve, and Wenger was quick to come to the defence of the teenager from the Paris suburb of Trappes. But he knew Anelka had to build up his body strength and get into

---

Stephen Hughes.

PUMA
JVC
28

more scoring positions. 'Nicolas still has some learning to do,' said Wenger at the end of January. 'He needs particularly to become more dangerous in the penalty area. At the moment, he doesn't get in the box enough.'

A fortnight later, Wenger sensed improvement. 'He's getting better with every match. He has improved his fighting spirit. He's growing used to English football, and it shows in his form. It's easy to forget he's still only eighteen. It's important that our crowd supports such young players.' (Anelka turned nineteen on 14 March.) Tony Adams shared Wenger's optimism. 'With Wrighty injured, Nicolas knew he was going to get a run and I think he's benefited from being able to play without pressure. He's coming on fast.'

In the goalless draw at West Ham, Anelka even operated as a lone striker. A few days later he was called into France's full squad for the first time. Two goals in the 3–1 win over Newcastle, followed by one of his 'specials' at Blackburn – running on to Nigel Winterburn's through ball at searing pace to shred the cover – lifted his confidence even higher. By Wembley he had developed the upper-body power to hold off tough challenges. He had cultivated greater awareness of the players around him and he'd shown how effectively he could finish. One of his biggest tasks next season will be to time his runs to avoid being caught offside. It will be a test too, how he reacts to the disappointment of not making France's final World Cup squad. But Wenger has no doubts. 'Earlier in the season, Nicolas lacked confidence because he had no experience of high-level competition. Now he has made the adjustment. He has shown the mental strength necessary to succeed and he can go on to become a world-class striker.'

'I feel more settled now,' said Anelka, a near neighbour of Patrick Vieira in Edgware. It showed: the youngest, and shyest, of Arsenal's French imports had

Nicolas Anelka scores Arsenal's fourth goal at Blackburn before the snows came.

grown remarkably in stature. His rise was symbolic of Arsenal's transformation after Christmas. It also symbolised the contribution made by players who started the season as young reserves.

The fans already knew about England Under-21 midfielder Stephen Hughes, one of the stars of Arsenal's 1994 FA Youth Cup winners. Hughes stayed in the shadows during the early part of the season. But the left-footed midfielder played a vital role after Christmas, deputising first for Patrick Vieira, then Manu Petit, or coming on as a substitute. Hughes converted the Gunners' final penalty in the shoot-out at Port Vale. His two goals killed off Chelsea, then second in the table, on 8 February. And Hughes's assist set up Chris Wreh to crack the winner at Bolton.

Hughes was always ready to take responsibility, in open play or at dead ball kicks. The key question was: would he agree a new contract to stay at Highbury? Hughes answered that in February by signing a five-year deal. 'He is a very talented player and I think he has a very good future at the club,' said Wenger, who felt Hughes's stamina level increased with every game at top level. 'Arsenal want to be the best and I want to play with the best,' said Hughes. 'Competition for places is part of that. I have confidence in my own ability and I believe I can rise to the challenge.'

Wreh, the Liberian international, came good in the New Year too. Before Christmas he seemed an unlikely hero. If Arsenal fans thought of him at all, it was usually as the substitute who missed a glorious chance in the last minute of the 3–2 win over Manchester United. But when Wreh started his first league game at Selhurst Park on 11 March, he made an immediate impact, scoring the winner against Wimbledon that put the Gunners in good heart for their crucial trip to Old Trafford. One paper neatly summed up the value of that goal: 'A Wreh of Hope.'

Christopher Wreh's trademark somersault after scoring against Wimbledon.

'It was important for me to score that night, to repay the faith the manager had shown in me and to show the fans what I could do,' said twenty-two-year-old Wreh.

'Starting the match enabled me to settle and be up with the pace straight away, whereas it's harder as a substitute, coming on and trying to adjust. Hopefully my performance answered some of the fans' questions.'

Suddenly he was more than a 'Wreh of hope'; he had become an influential deputy for Dennis Bergkamp. Wreh's stinging twenty-yarder which settled a tense match at Bolton stoked up the pressure on Manchester United. 'That was vital,' said Adams. 'It was one of our games in hand on United and we had to make it count.' And five days later, Wreh tucked away Vieira's pass for the semi-final winner against Wolves.

Wenger had signed the teenage Wreh for Monaco on George Weah's recommendation. 'He was the leading scorer among France's Under-17s and I followed his progress after I left Monaco,' said Wenger. 'I thought he was a great bargain when we signed him last summer. Two months ago, he was unknown outside Highbury. Since then, he has grown and grown in confidence. A successful team needs four good strikers in the squad. Nicolas Anelka and Chris Wreh give us that back-up.'

At the start of the season, Matthew Upson forecast: 'I know it's going to take time for me to break through.' By May, the nineteen-year-old defender had made four Premiership appearances, two covering for Nigel Winterburn, plus two more in his preferred position at centre-back. Like Anelka, he has natural pace. Like Anelka, he built up his body strength in the gym so he could resist physical strikers like Hartson. Adams, for one, expects more from Upson in 1998–99.

Luis Boa Morte was a frequent sub, using his speed to run at tiring defenders. Arsenal's Premier Youth League captain Paolo Vernazza made an exacting league debut as a makeshift Gunners side squeezed out the 1–0 victory over Crystal Palace that kept the winning run going.

Then there was Alex Manninger. When David Seaman broke a finger at Coventry in January, Wenger called up the then twenty-year-old Austrian ahead of John Lukic. Manninger had already distinguished himself in the Coca-Cola Cup win over Coventry. Said Wenger: 'He is a very confident young goalkeeper – though maybe a little audacious!' Lukic himself described Manninger as 'the best goalkeeper I've seen at that age'. Goalkeeping coach Bob Wilson agreed. 'Alex is a natural gymnast, with tremendous natural ability. He's one of the keenest trainers I've ever seen. He's a real diamond, and sometimes I have to pinch myself to realise how young he is.'

Manninger quickly showed his quality in the last half hour of the FA Cup tie at Middlesbrough, when he pulled off a string of athletic saves to foil a Boro comeback. 'It was a big game for me,' he said. 'As a keeper, you need to stop shots and take crosses, but decision-making is even more important. That part of your game improves with experience and the Boro match was most valuable to me for that reason.'

Manninger's ability to catch centres – despite Mark Hughes's Coca-Cola semi-final goal – fuelled his self-belief. 'Goalkeepers in England have to deal with far more crosses

Christopher Wreh, Remi Garde and Luis Boa Morte congratulate Alex Manninger after the FA Cup quarter-final shoot-out at West Ham.

than goalkeepers anywhere else in Europe. After making some good catches, I settled down and felt strong coming for the ball.'

He made some vital saves too: from Simon Rodger against Palace; in the second half against Wimbledon at Selhurst Park; the block that denied Andy Cole at Old Trafford; stops from Eyal Berkovic in both games of the FA Cup quarter-final against West Ham. It was Manninger's save from the Israeli international that turned the penalty shoot-out Arsenal's way. By the time Seaman was fit to return, Manninger had already been named Carling Player of the Month for March. 'He's a young man with an excellent future,' commented Lukic. 'I'm sure he'll become a great goalkeeper.'

Arsenal also possessed hugely experienced cover in David Platt and Gilles Grimandi. 'This time, we had big back-up,' said Wenger. But the Gunners' young players provided a lot of back-up themselves. As Wilson said: 'The players who stepped in did so much towards Arsenal's success – and no other club could match that.'

JVC
JVC

ONE GAME AT A TIME

'One day at a time' runs the title of the famous country song. Arsenal changed it to 'One game at a time' on the title run-in. The players took their cue from Arsène Wenger and Tony Adams. 'We must be very focused,' said the manager, as Sheffield Wednesday came to Highbury on 28 March. Eight days later, Arsenal were due to meet Wolves in the FA Cup semi-final at Villa Park. No one would have guessed, from the mood of the players. Said Adams: 'I won't start thinking about that until next Wednesday, because today's game – and the one at Bolton on Tuesday – are so vital to our Championship chances.'

David Seaman, recovered from his finger injury, was back in goal. Wednesday gave him one of his quieter afternoons. Arsenal created chance after chance, but only took one. After thirty-five minutes Marc Overmars prised open the Owls' defence and fed Dennis Bergkamp, who finished low and true from close range. Another 'one-nil to the Arsenal', though the result flattered Ron Atkinson's side. At Old Trafford, United had beaten Wimbledon 2–0.

Tuesday night at Bolton's packed Reebok Stadium was a battle. Both teams desperately needed the points: the Gunners to chase the title; Wanderers to avoid relegation. It was a hairy night. Seaman was at his best throughout, making vital saves from Alan Thompson and Nathan Blake. 'That's David Seaman,' said Bob Wilson. 'The best goalies make the fewest mistakes – and they make match-winning saves which inspire their own side and deflate the opposition.'

'David always has the air of a man in control,' said John Lukic. 'His self-belief unhinges attackers. How laid back he really is behind that big grin, maybe only David knows!'

Arsenal defended as though their lives depended on it. They played the last twenty-seven minutes with ten men after referee Keith Burge red-carded Martin Keown for a second bookable offence when he hauled back Blake. A few minutes earlier, Chris

Manu Petit offers up a prayer of thanks after his first goal for Arsenal, against Wimbledon.

Patrick Vieira cracks a spectacular shot for the third goal against Newcastle.

Wreh had blasted the only goal. Manu Petit and sub Stephen Hughes combined on the left. Hughes found Wreh on the edge of the box and the Liberian striker unleashed a stinging right foot shot past Keith Branagan, before rushing into the now-familiar somersault. 'I'd heard Chris was a good player who thrives on confidence,' said Adams. 'His confidence must be sky high now, after scoring the winners at Wimbledon and Bolton.' Steve Bould came on to replace Keown and Wenger left just one up front. But Arsenal held out. 'Even when they were down to ten, they made it hard for us,' said Bolton manager Colin Todd.

'I don't want to keep winning one-nil,' said Wenger, after Arsenal had seen off Wolves by the familiar scoreline – Wreh's goal again – in the semi-final. 'I'd much rather win five-nil. It would be better for my nerves.' But Wenger knew he had battle-hardened players who'd won trophies before Seaman, Lee Dixon, Adams, Bould and Nigel Winterburn had played in Arsenal Championship teams. Bergkamp and Overmars had won everything going with

Ajax. Petit had gained a French title medal with Monaco the year before. Arsenal didn't score five when Newcastle – their Wembley opponents – came to Highbury on Easter Saturday, 11 April. But 3–1 did nicely.

The day after the Gunners reached Wembley, United had come from behind to beat Blackburn 3–1 at Ewood Park. Andy Cole, Paul Scholes and David Beckham scored as United turned up the power in the second half. That left the Gunners six points behind Alex Ferguson's team, with three games in hand. Fergie was quick to point out again that Arsenal still needed seven points to go top, because of United's superior goal difference. Adams – who doesn't have Sky at home – didn't even watch the match. 'I didn't see any reason, because I believe what we have to do is in our hands,' he explained.

And Newcastle? 'This match has no relevance to Wembley,' Adams said. 'The circumstances will be totally different. We need three points towards the Championship. We may have to be patient to open them up.' Nicolas Anelka smashed a twenty-yarder four minutes before half time to make the vital breakthrough. Ray Parlour's cross set up Anelka for his second. Then Patrick Vieira lashed a brutal twenty-five-yarder past Shay Given – more spectacular even than his Highbury strike against United. 'The best goal I've scored for Arsenal!' beamed Vieira. Warren Barton, Stoke Newington-born and a Gunners fan as a boy, scored the first league goal against Arsenal since 17 January. 'It was typical of the players that afterwards, they were disappointed because we had conceded a goal,' said Wenger.

Next day, Liverpool, clearly hyped up for the occasion, held United 1–1 at Old Trafford. Ronny Johnsen gave United a twelfth-minute lead, wiped out by Michael Owen who then got himself sent off for the second of two bookable tackles, rising to the bait after a string of 'verbals'.

United didn't have a game on Easter Monday. Arsenal's match at Blackburn kicked off late again for Sky. It was a freezing night, warmed by the pace of Arsenal's football. Barely seventy-five seconds had gone when Bergkamp, back after a three-match suspension, hared clear to beat Alan Fettis. Ray Parlour cracked Arsenal's second five minutes later and the game was dead by the fourteenth minute, when Fettis palmed out Bergkamp's shot and Parlour smacked in the rebound. As half time approached, Anelka raced on to Winterburn's through ball, outpaced Rovers' cover and calmly tucked his shot past Fettis. Kevin Gallacher's second-half volley was merely a consolation for Blackburn, as Arsenal's travelling thousands released bunches of red balloons to compete with the falling snow. Sky's chart showed Arsenal only had 48 per cent of the possession, which just shows how dangerous statistics can be.

After the game, Bergkamp talked about the Gunners' potential; how this team could go on to play in the style of Ajax's great sides. Now Arsenal were one point behind United, with two games in hand. Fergie – and the bookmakers – installed Arsenal as title favourites. The tabloids who'd lambasted the Gunners at Christmas now queued up to acclaim 'Arsène's Awesome Arsenal'. Wenger was having none of it. Wimbledon, the great party poopers, were next at Highbury. 'It's very important that we focus totally on the game ahead,' said Wenger. 'That's the key to playing well and being successful. We must keep our concentration and I know that idea is present in the minds of all our players. Wimbledon are a strong side who enjoy making life difficult for the big clubs. That's another good reason why we must be totally focused.'

Wenger was equally matter-of-fact about the 'favourites' label. 'It's far better to be favourites than to be nowhere. But the label means little to us. Three months ago, many people said the race was for second place. We didn't listen then, and we shan't listen to the hype now.'

Wenger's remarkable calmness spread throughout the dressing room – and the crowd. Even the fans were repeating 'one game at a time' like a mantra. Adams summed up: 'The mathematics are simple. United can take twelve points from their last four games and they have a superior goal difference. So we need fourteen points from our last six matches to win the Championship.'

Wimbledon were a bogey team to Arsenal. The Dons hadn't lost at Highbury for nine seasons; but Arsenal destroyed them that afternoon. Adams started the rout with a flying twelfth-minute header. By the twentieth minute, Overmars and Bergkamp had made it 3–0. Petit then celebrated his first goal for the Gunners. 'I knew it was only a matter of time before Manu scored because he's been getting into good positions,' said Wenger. Sub Wreh lobbed Neil Sullivan to head the fifth. 'Five-nil to the Arsenal.'

Meanwhile, Newcastle held United 1–1 at Old Trafford. Swedish striker Andreas Andersson picked a glorious moment to score his first league goal in England. David Beckham equalised, but United couldn't add a second. It was a decisive afternoon. The mathematics were even simpler now. The Gunners led United by one point, with two games in hand. And they were still taking one game at a time. As Lee Dixon said: 'We say "well done", then we go home. We've won nothing yet.'

The following Saturday, Arsenal were away to another side fighting relegation: Barnsley. The Gunners' 1,950 seat tickets had sold like hot cakes. More than 12,000 – a Highbury record – packed the North Bank stand for the 'beam back' from Oakwell. Barnsley oozed determination. But Bergkamp turned the game again. His twenty-third minute curler, with virtually no backlift, was the stuff of dreams. 'That's the beauty of great players,' said Wenger. 'Dennis took the shot so quickly the defenders had no time to react. That goal gave us a chance to settle down and take command.'

But Wenger grew pensive as the Gunners failed to kill the game – Seaman even had to pull off some diving saves – until Overmars pounced on David Platt's pass and drilled a low shot past David Watson to make it 2–0. 'Marc's goal made the game safe and that was a relief,' said Wenger. 'Against a team like Barnsley, who were battling to survive in the Premiership, we needed that second goal to give us a cushion.'

The home fans even applauded Arsenal off the pitch. 'We're not accustomed to having an opposition crowd clapping and waving at us!' said Martin Keown. 'They'd seen their team beaten and fall further into relegation trouble, but they appreciated the way we played.' Wenger praised the Gunners' concentration. He was also keen to stress the depth of Arsenal's squad. Platt had replaced the suspended Parlour at Oakwell. Bould, Lukic, Gilles Grimandi, Stephen Hughes and Wreh were on the bench: a lot of talent to call on if needed.

United demolished bottom club Palace 3–0 at Selhurst Park two days later. But it was all in Arsenal's hands now. Two wins – at home to Derby and Everton – and the title would be on its way to Highbury. Derby, the Gunners' midweek opponents, had crashed 0–4 at home to Leicester the

Dennis Bergkamp scores at Blackburn after seventy-five seconds.

Ray Parlour nets his second at Blackburn.

previous Sunday. 'They've got pride to play for, and they'll make things tough for us,' forecast Adams.

Jim Smith obviously had told his side a few home truths. They spent the first half hassling Arsenal all over Highbury. Bergkamp had a penalty saved, then limped off with a pulled hamstring which would keep him out for the rest of the domestic season. But Petit, so influential since Christmas, decided the game after thirty-four minutes. Overmars won the ball back on the edge of the box and slipped a short pass to

the Frenchman, who crashed a left-foot shot beyond Mart Poom. Petit almost scored twice more with long range second-half shots. 'He's on a roll right now,' grinned Adams.

That second half seemed to drag on for ages. It was a relieved bunch of Gunners, both players and supporters, who celebrated when referee Neale Barry blew the final whistle. 'It wasn't a time for silky football. We had to put a foot in and compete – which we did,' said Adams.

Victory over Everton on Sunday and the title was Arsenal's. But 'one game at a time': Wenger said it again. 'Our attitude has always been to concentrate on winning the next match. In that sense, nothing has changed for today's game.'

An own goal by Slaven Bilic under pressure from Adams gave Arsenal the early breakthrough. Overmars, electric on the day, raced away to beat Thomas Myrhe for the second. Everton targeted Petit. John O'Kane clobbered him just before Overmars's goal, then Don Hutchison's lunge knocked him out of the game. Enter Platt. The flying Overmars, and Adams – converting Steve Bould's inch-perfect pass – turned Highbury into a joyous carnival of flags, banners and inflatable trophies.

Each and every player in the squad, and Wenger's coaching staff, came out to lift the Championship trophy before an ecstatic crowd. The cheers for Bergkamp could be heard in Muswell Hill. So could those for Wenger. Forget the meaningless results at Liverpool and Aston Villa to come; Arsenal had won the title with two games to spare. In 1971 and 1989, the title race had gone to the last gasp of the last game. In 1991, George Graham's Gunners won with two games left. The crowd that Monday night partied right through a 3–1 win over Manchester United. That was a May bank holiday weekend too. Now the Arsenal fans would party again – one night at a time.

BERGKAMP

'Which planet does he come from?' Louis van Gaal used to ask regularly when he was at Ajax. Van Gaal went on to win the Champions League with Ajax and last season won the Spanish Championship with Barcelona. The man he was talking about didn't do badly either. Double winner; Footballer of the Year; PFA Player of the Year; equal top European (with Zinedine Zidane) in UEFA's World Player of the Year poll; the first player ever to score all three top goals in *Match of the Day*'s 'Goal of the Month' award . . . the boy Bergkamp done great. 'When I was at Ajax,' said Van Gaal, 'I used to tell people that Dennis came from another planet. He can't be of this world, with his qualities. He has it in him to become bigger even than Marco van Basten and Ruud Gullit.'

Bergkamp won trophies galore with Ajax. Then he spent two unhappy years with Inter in Serie A, before joining the Gunners. 'Is Dennis a midfielder or a forward?' smiled Bruce Rioch when Bergkamp arrived. 'He's neither. He likes to attack from just behind the main striker.' Maybe that was part of Bergkamp's problem in Italy. Ex-Holland coach Dick Advocaat summed Bergkamp up: 'He is a player who can score at any time, in any game. He also has the ability to fit in anywhere in attack, wherever any coach wants him to play.' Inter wanted him to play up front – sometimes alone – where the marking was fiercest. Even so, Bergkamp's goals were crucial to Inter's 1994 UEFA Cup success.

Said Bergkamp: 'I had the feeling in Italy that players were given roles to play where they didn't develop. They had to do a certain job, which didn't always bring out their best qualities. It's different with Arsène Wenger. He likes to use players in roles where they can improve. That's been good for all of us.'

Rioch, then Wenger, freed Bergkamp to do what he does best: attack from deeper positions. Don Howe, who describes Bergkamp as 'a Rolls Royce of a player'

Dennis Bergkamp voted third equal in FIFA's 1997 World Player of the Year awards behind Ronaldo and Roberto Carlos, and alongside Zinedine Zidane.

adidas
THE GUNNERS
Arsenal
JVC

summed up his special ability: 'His movement makes it very hard for defenders to pick him up. He poses so many questions. Do you man-mark him? Does a defender follow him? Or does a midfield player drop back?' Few opponents have come up with a concrete solution. 'I like to play behind the front man and that makes it more difficult for defenders to track me, especially if they're playing a flat back four, because they may not want to follow me if I drop deep,' said Bergkamp. 'I think my biggest strength is my pace, with or without the ball, and that helps me cause defenders problems.'

When Bergkamp came to Highbury, north London was in the grip of its first bout of Klinsmania. At the time, Tony Adams forecast: 'Dennis will make a bigger impact than just about any other foreign signing. Defenders will have their hands full coping with him. He reminds me of Kenny Dalglish, because he doesn't just score goals, he makes them for others. I'm glad I only have to mark him in training.' Nearly three years later, Adams smiles at his prescience. 'It was one of the easiest forecasts I've ever had to make,' he said.

Season 1997–98 was Bergkamp's finest for Arsenal, even if that hamstring injury against Derby did keep him out of the FA Cup final and the Championship clincher against Everton. 'At Ajax, I missed one leg of the UEFA Cup final because I was ill,' said Bergkamp when he was ruled out for Wembley. 'This time I hoped I would be fit. I sat out the Everton match when we won the Championship, which was our most important league match of the year. Now I must miss the FA Cup final. As a small boy I watched the final and dreamed about playing in it, so it's hard for me to take. I want to be remembered as a player who helps his team win trophies.'

Bergkamp's disappointment shows his commitment to Arsenal. He is no mercenary, here for the money and already thinking of his next transfer. On match days, wife Henrita brings along young daughter Estelle, clad in an Arsenal number 10 shirt, with 'Dad' on the back. The Bergkamp family are settled in Hertfordshire. Maybe Dennis will even finish his career at Highbury. Such things matter to supporters.

Bergkamp at some times appears the least emotional of players. But he cares, all right. As Adams said: 'Different people have different ways of showing their feelings. Dennis doesn't make a big thing of it, but he always wants to win, desperately.'

In an age when some stars' careers have become soap operas, Bergkamp stands apart. Nightclub booze-ups, flash cars and gold medallions: they're miles from Bergkamp. 'He has a strong family life and he is dedicated to making himself the best player he possibly can be,' said Wenger.

Pat Rice was Arsenal's youth coach when Bergkamp arrived. He used to tell his boys to go and watch the Dutchman in training, because 'they could pick up so much from just watching him'. Now Wenger's assistant, Rice still holds up Bergkamp as the ideal role model. 'Everyone can learn from his technique and dedication.'

Not that Bergkamp is a total goody-goody. He was kicked from pillar to post throughout 1997–98, and occasionally he retaliated – like when he swung his elbow back into Steve Lomas in the FA Cup tie at West Ham. Mostly though, Bergkamp was more sinned against than sinner. It's strange: in this country, despite all the directives from FIFA and UEFA, players of Bergkamp's calibre are expected to absorb the brutality dished out to them like latter-day saints. When Bergkamp finally exploded, he was the one on the wrong end of the referee's cards. The goalless draw at Crystal Palace in October was a prize example. Hermann Hreidarsson spent ninety minutes tugging, obstructing and fouling Bergkamp. But referee Steve Dunn yellow-carded Bergkamp, earning him a three-match suspension. Alan Smith, booked just once in his long career, summed up the absurdity of the situation. 'Answers have to be found when a player as mild-mannered as Dennis Bergkamp is about to begin a three-match ban and we're little more than two months into the season.'

Said Adams: 'I feel for Dennis because he's a marked man. Even calm characters

Dennis Bergkamp races away to open the score at Blackburn.

can be provoked if they're hassled for long enough. I hope referees will realise what's going on and give Dennis some protection.' Some hope. Wenger spent most of the season pleading for referees to protect Bergkamp, but to no avail. As Wenger said after Bergkamp's hamstring injury against Derby: 'He pulled it stretching for the ball while his shirt was being tugged.'

Yet Bergkamp has developed physically after two years in England. 'My first season was difficult because I had to get used to the demands of Premiership football. In 1996, I was injured in the pre-season preparations and I wasn't able to apply myself fully for a while after the start of the season. In 1997, everything came together for me.' As Sky analyst Andy Gray said: 'He's stronger-minded, and physically stronger, than he's ever been.'

Bergkamp's start to the season was magnificent. Two goals in the 3–1 win at Southampton were followed by a stunning hat trick in the 3–3 draw at Leicester. Bergkamp's third, when he lobbed over Matt Elliott and then beat Kasey Keller, was the stuff of dreams. 'It was like when I played as a boy,' said Bergkamp. 'I would hear the commentator: "The ball comes to Bergkamp. He takes it on. He shoots. Bergkamp . . . It's a goal for Bergkamp!"'

Tom Watt, the actor, writer and Arsenal fanatic, said it all. 'It was an emotional roller-coaster of a game. We should have won it. But what can you say about Dennis Bergkamp? Football doesn't come any better than Dennis's hat trick!' 'Fantastic, world class,' added Wenger.

How many more magic moments did Bergkamp provide? Memorable home goals against Bolton and Barnsley for a start. Goals for Ian Wright. Deft passes to release his old

Dennis Bergkamp on the way to completing his hat trick at Leicester.

Dennis Bergkamp curls a vital goal at Barnsley.

friend Marc Overmars, Nicolas Anelka and Chris Wreh.

Bergkamp was at the peak of his form when he was suspended. English football's disciplinary regulations allowed him to come back and score the winner in the Coca-Cola Cup against Coventry while he was banned from league action. But the suspension took its toll. 'It was hard for me mentally, because I was very happy with my form and then suddenly I wasn't able to play. I felt helpless. I wanted to be out there, but I couldn't be. No one can keep their form for five weeks without playing. Yes, you keep up fitness levels, but you only find your rhythm playing games.' It took Bergkamp a little while. But by February, Wenger was warning: 'I think Dennis is close to his best again.'

Another suspension intervened after Bergkamp's red card at West Ham, though he scored a vital winner against Sheffield Wednesday at Highbury in his last game before the ban. His return was sensational. First, he charged away to score in seventy-five seconds and set the Gunners up to rip Blackburn apart 4–1. He netted again in the 5–0 slaughter of Wimbledon. Then, at Barnsley, he curled an amazing shot past David Watson for the goal that gave Arsenal control. Hardly any movement, hardly any backlift, but Bergkamp generated enough power to beat the keeper from twenty yards.

'Such technique,' said Wenger.

'We're walking in a Bergkamp wonderland,' sang the fans.

But that's Bergkamp: a great player who turns vital matches.

THE COCA-COLA CUP

When is a weakened team not a weakened team? When it wins 4–1 in the third round of the Coca-Cola Cup. That was the start of the Gunners' run in the only major domestic competition they didn't win. It was a run to the brink of Wembley that evolved almost by accident, only to end in a semi-final cauldron of emotion at Stamford Bridge.

Birmingham, from Nationwide Division One, were the Highbury visitors for that third round tie on 14 October. Arsenal fielded a seriously weakened side; Lee Dixon and David Platt were the only regulars in the starting line-up. Elsewhere, Manchester United were doing something very similar – and clearing the decks for their Champions League campaign by losing 0–2 at Ipswich. But there was no European dimension for the Gunners. They'd already gone out of the UEFA Cup to PAOK Salonika. Arsène Wenger explained: 'We had twelve players away on international duty last week. Some couldn't even train before the Birmingham match. That's why I rested so many senior players.'

Luis Boa Morte celebrates his first goal against Birmingham.

The team lined up: Manninger; Dixon, Marshall, Grimandi, Upson; Mendez, Platt, Vernazza, Hughes; Wreh, Boa Morte. Alex Manninger, Matthew Upson, Alberto Mendez, Paolo Vernazza and Chris Wreh were all making their competitive debuts for the Gunners. So was sub Jason Crowe, who was red-carded a minute after coming on, joining the Blues' Darren Wassall, sent off by Uriah Rennie six minutes from the end of normal time.

A crowd of 27,097 watched at first with scepticism and then cheered themselves hoarse as Luis Boa Morte equalised Tony Hey's goal for Birmingham and the Gunners ran riot in extra time. Platt, from the penalty spot, Boa Morte (again) and Mendez scored to force a significant win. Significant not just because Arsenal had reached the fourth round, but because the youngsters had demonstrated the depth of Wenger's back-up resources. 'It was a big reward for me, to see so many happy faces

Luis Boa Morte hits his second goal against Birmingham.

at the end,' said Wenger. 'I enjoyed the performance because all the players showed real Arsenal spirit.'

'The youngsters benefited from having experienced players like Lee and David around,' said Adams, who admitted he'd been glad of the break. 'But it's rare that we've been able to field such a strong back-up team. Even two years ago, we couldn't have put out so many young players and still been confident of winning. That shows how Arsène Wenger has strengthened the squad.'

Wenger fielded another hybrid team when Coventry visited Highbury in the fourth round. Dennis Bergkamp was suspended for three Premiership games, but under England's arcane disciplinary system he was free to play in the Coca-Cola Cup. It gave him valuable match practice during his league ban. Steve Bould, suspended against Birmingham, returned. So did Martin Keown, after his summer injury in Le Tournoi. Ray Parlour beefed up the midfield. But Manu Petit was suspended and Wenger rested David Seaman, Nigel Winterburn, Tony Adams, Patrick Vieira, Marc Overmars and Ian Wright. Arsenal needed extra time again and Bergkamp, coolly slipping the ball past Steve Ogrizovic, to beat Gordon Strachan's much-improved side.

Now things were getting serious. The Football League were pressing UEFA to restore the Coca-Cola Cup winners' automatic place in the UEFA Cup. And at the turn of the year, the Coca-Cola Cup looked a handy fail-safe route into Europe for the Gunners.

The quarter-final at West Ham fell on a rain-sodden night. The Hammers did well to get the game played at all. Adams watched via satellite from the south of France. Ex-Gunner John Hartson wanted to make a big impression against his old club. Instead, Seaman saved his penalty that could have put West Ham ahead. 'David knows John's game very well and I think that put John at a disadvantage,' said Wenger. Then the Welsh striker subsided under stern marking from Keown and Bould. Ian

Wright made a quick impression on his return from suspension, firing home a Bergkamp pass to give Arsenal the lead. It was to be Wright's last first-team goal of the season. Eight days later, in the FA Cup replay at Port Vale, Arsenal's record scorer suffered the first of a series of injuries that kept him out for nearly four months.

In the second half, Overmars – skating over the wet top – grew more dangerous by the minute. When he scored the decisive second goal, he was serving notice of things to come. So was Keown, who had another outstanding game. Samassi Abou pulled one back, but Arsenal held on. The 2–1 win was just what Arsenal needed, after their problems in the league and the goalless third round FA Cup draw against Port Vale. Now Wembley's towers were on the horizon.

The semi-final matched Arsenal against Chelsea. Patrick Vieira was away with the French squad. Seaman, Dixon and Keown were all injured. Bergkamp almost gave Arsenal an early lead – then Overmars did. Ruud Gullit's team selection seemed to have handed the initiative to Arsenal. When Stephen Hughes lashed home Overmars's cross to make it 2–0 early in the second half, the Highbury fans dreamed of Wembley. Instead, the Gunners missed chances and Chelsea keeper Ed de Goey was inspired. Then Gullit, prodded by his assistant, ex-Gunner Graham Rix, sent on Mark Hughes. Within minutes, 'Sparky' had nipped in front of Manninger to head a vital away goal.

Marc Overmars puts Arsenal ahead in the semi-final first leg against Chelsea.

Wenger was disappointed with the 2–1 scoreline. 'We dropped our level towards the end of the game,' he said. 'We should have killed the game at 2–0. Chelsea's goal upset me. Manninger made a typical mistake that inexperienced goalkeepers make. But we made five mistakes throughout that Chelsea move, and I hate it when we concede a goal even though we outnumber our opponents.'

In between the first and second legs, Wright was seeing surgeons – and Chelsea sacked Gullit as manager. The second leg at Stamford Bridge was Gianluca Vialli's first home game in charge. It was a night of huge emotion. Arsenal were without the injured Bould, and Adams remembered: 'We missed him. On nights like that, you want your most experienced players on the pitch.'

Mark Hughes spent the first ten minutes trying to sort out Arsenal's defenders. That typified Chelsea's approach. Chelsea were already one up, through Hughes, when Vieira was sent off after felling Dennis Wise and collecting a red card from Graham Poll for his second bookable offence. 'That was a turning point,' said Wenger. 'With eleven men, I felt we could have got a result. With ten, it was impossible. We hardly had any time to reorganise before they scored their second goal. That was a crucial point in the match.' Bergkamp's penalty in the eighty-third minute, after Chelsea had taken a 3–0 lead, came too late to spark an Arsenal revival.

'I think it was the first game at Highbury that won it for us and we can take no credit for that,' said Rix. 'Despite getting a mauling, we only went down 1–2, and scored an important away goal which always gives you a chance. 4–1 wouldn't have flattered Arsenal. They should have buried us that night. But everything that happened behind the scenes at Chelsea between then and the second leg swung the impetus our way. We'd already decided we had to have a

Stephen Hughes nets Arsenal's second in the semi-final first leg.

go at Arsenal and everyone was so pumped up because of the Gullit/Vialli situation. The circumstances were right for us,' added Rix, before forecasting: 'But Arsenal won't lose many games.'

'It was a huge disappointment,' said Adams. 'Chelsea were really fired up. But we should have done better. We had to dig in and I felt we lost some of our discipline. It must have been a very frustrating night for our fans. The only way we can respond is by bouncing back and beating Palace in the league on Saturday. That would lift our confidence and convince people that we have the mental strength to get over disappointments.'

Arsenal scraped home 1–0 against Palace with a makeshift team, and the rest of that amazing Championship run is history. 'We learned from that night at Stamford Bridge,' reflected Adams. 'We kept it in our minds – and told ourselves that we didn't want to get beaten like that again . . .'

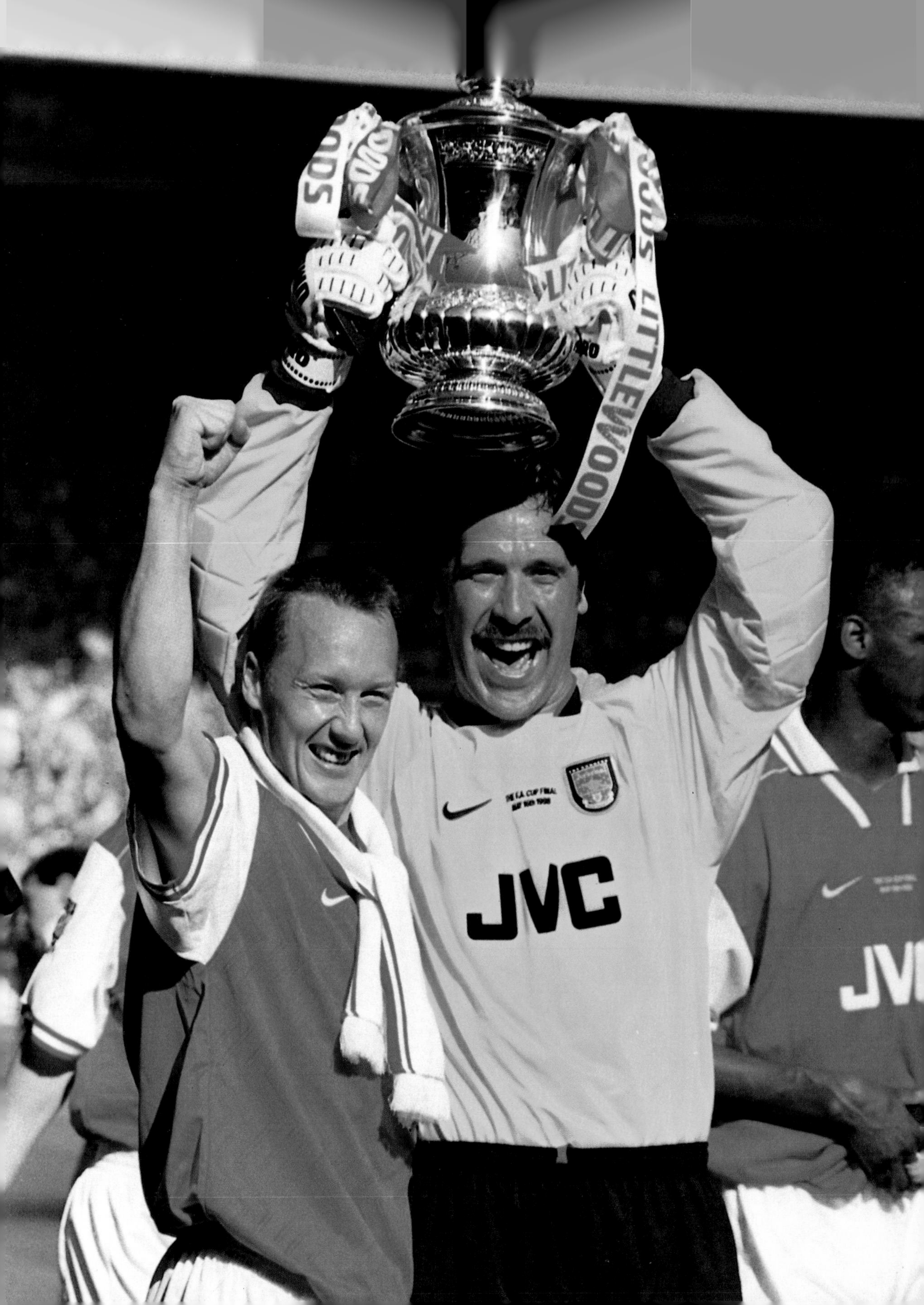
LITTLEWOODS
JVC

THE FA CUP

Tony Adams had lifted the FA Cup from the Duchess of Kent. The Gunners danced on the pitch, while the fans went potty. Even the sun that tanned Wembley's sweltering thousands seemed to be shining on Arsenal.

It was all so different back in January. Arsenal met struggling Nationwide Division One side Port Vale in the third round at Highbury. Easy for the Gunners on paper, but football isn't played on paper. Arsenal huffed and puffed but couldn't break Vale down. The Nationwide club escaped with a goalless draw, and a chance to stun the Gunners in the replay.

'We were struggling to remember when we'd last won a game,' recalled Vale manager John Rudge. 'We hadn't won in seven weeks and we'd slipped from seventh to eighteenth in the division. But we gave a great defensive performance. Everyone was really committed. We were well-organised and defended particularly well at set plays.'

Lee Dixon and David Seaman with the FA Cup.

To fuel the Highbury fans' frustration, the PA announcer read out scores from other ties: 'West Ham 2, Emley 1. The scorer of the winning goal was John Hartson.' It was like a hammer blow, while Nicolas Anelka was struggling to transfer his natural talent into bruising match situations. He would answer more fully at Wembley.

In the *Daily Telegraph*, Alan Smith documented the views of many fans. 'At a time when Arsenal goals are hard to come by – only five in the last seven games – news of Hartson's goal was the last thing the Highbury faithful wanted to hear. Many supporters are now questioning the wisdom of Arsène Wenger's decision to allow both Hartson and Paul Merson to leave.'

In the *Sun*, Brian Woolnough wrote: 'Massive problems are mounting up for Arsenal. And they were easily exposed by First Division Port Vale. For a start, Arsène Wenger's side have forgotten how to score. The defence is too old, there are no youngsters emerging, and Wenger's fringe signings, like Gilles Grimandi, are not good enough. Crisis? Not yet – but there will be at the end of the season, when Wenger has to be ruthless. We shall then be able to examine how good this particular foreign coach is. Wenger is under pressure. First he has to carry this Arsenal side – half of them too old, others not good enough – to a trophy this season. Then he must ruthlessly leave behind the old Arsenal and build a new one – before it's too late for him and the famous club.'

Wenger, though, isn't one to hold a grudge. When Woolnough asked him about contract negotiations after the Cup final, Wenger joked: 'Do you want to be my agent? Shall I give you ten per cent?'

The replay was equally hairy. The Wembley dream almost died before it had begun. Ian Wright had a goal disallowed and Marc Overmars hit the woodwork, but the score remained 0–0 after ninety minutes. On to extra time. Dennis Bergkamp produced a piece of magic, a wondrous lob from twenty-five yards, to put Arsenal ahead. But that didn't break Vale's spirit. With eight minutes left, Wayne Corden touched home Gareth Ainsworth's cross.

It was all down to the lottery of penalties. The Gunners had one great advantage: David Seaman, England's Euro 96 hero, in goal. As Wenger said: 'His physical presence makes it very difficult for him to be beaten. The pressure is on players who face him in shoot-outs.' But when Paul Musselwhite saved Lee Dixon's spot kick, it was Vale who held the psychological advantage. On the touchline, Wenger was brooding. 'At that stage, I thought there was a sixty per cent chance we'd lose,' he admitted. 'When you miss the first shot, you don't usually come back.'

David Seaman's vital save in the penalty shoot-out at Port Vale in the third round replay.

Ray Parlour and Bergkamp scored for Arsenal. It was 2–2 on kicks when Ian Bogie stepped up to take Vale's third penalty. Seaman flung himself to save. The pressure was back on the men from the Potteries. Luis Boa Morte and Stephen Hughes made certain from the spot. Vale trailed 3–4 when Allen Tankard ran up to strike their fifth penalty. Maybe, intimidated by Seaman's towering presence, he blasted over the bar. It was cruel finale for a defender who'd earlier kept his side in contention with a brilliant clearance to deny Bergkamp, four minutes before the Dutchman's goal. On such margins do Doubles depend. 'When the ball flew over the top, time just stood still for me,' said Tankard. 'I felt so alone. I was looking for a hole to jump into.'

So Arsenal went through to a fourth round tie at Middlesbrough. But the Gunners, knew they'd had a (very) narrow escape. And Boro meant Paul Merson, whose children – clad in Middlesbrough shirts over Arsenal tops – were mascots for the day.

The Gunners were superb in the first half. Overmars dispatched Bergkamp's piercing through ball to give Arsenal the lead after just sixty-eight seconds. Then Anelka's pass set up Parlour to shoot the second. 'We could have been six down at half time,' said Merson, who threw his shirt to the travelling Highbury fans at the final whistle. 'Arsenal played so well, and we made schoolboy errors.' But Merson struck for Boro, and the Gunners had to endure twenty-eight worrying minutes before progressing to the fifth round. Significantly, it was Tony Adams' first game back since his return from France. He wanted to praise Steve Bould though. 'As for us old 'uns, the way Bouldy played at Boro, he could go on for a little while yet . . .'

The fifth round pitted Arsenal against Crystal Palace. The game was a tragedy for Bould, who broke his arm after Bruce Dyer accidentally fell on him. Arsenal pressed and pressed, but couldn't find a decisive finish. Admitted Bergkamp: 'Palace made it difficult for us, but we were disappointed not to beat them.'

The game turned on two penalties that referee Martin Bodenham didn't give. Alex Manninger, deputising for the injured Seaman, brought down Jamie Fullarton and was booked. The referee gave the free kick outside the box. 'When I looked back at the video of the incident, it was inside the box and should have been a penalty,' admitted the Austrian keeper. At the other end, Palace escaped when Stephen Hughes was hauled down by Andy Roberts. Another goalless draw; another replay. At Selhurst Park, Anelka – growing in confidence with every game – lobbed Kevin Miller and headed home after just two minutes. Palace left-back Dean Gordon was sent off twenty minutes later. And Bergkamp rubbed salt into Palace's wounds by making it 2–0 from the free kick, deflected off Marc Edworthy. Bruce Dyer pulled one back, but it was too little too late. Overmars, flying in that afternoon after Holland's week in Florida, even made a twenty-minute substitute appearance. Manninger summed up: 'We had a bit of luck with Dennis's goal, but it was quite comfortable for us after that.'

Palace centre back Andy Linighan analysed most of the two games from the subs' bench. Said Arsenal's 1993 final hero: 'People may wonder how teams like Port Vale and Palace can go to Highbury and hold Arsenal. I think it has something to do with sides going there and simply setting out their stall to stop them and nick a draw. In the replay though, we had to come out and Arsenal had too much for us.' He added prophetically: 'Anelka is coming on in leaps and bounds.'

The quarter-final brought West Ham to Highbury. Twenty-three years earlier to the day a young striker called Alan Taylor had scored twice to earn the Hammers a 2–0 quarter-final victory at Arsenal. Adams was typically matter-of-fact. 'I've read about what happened then. Well, this is 1998 and the game is up for grabs.' Adams had also pinpointed Manninger as a potentially key figure. 'He reminds me of Boris Becker, the way he keeps talking to himself.'

West Ham were without the suspended Hartson and cup-tied Trevor Sinclair. They still took an early lead when Ian Pearce lashed a half-cleared corner back past Manninger – who then pulled off a vital save, denying Eyal Berkovic. Bergkamp levelled from the penalty spot after he'd been held in the box. West Ham strung nine and ten men behind the ball in the second half. Arsenal couldn't break through. That meant another replay.

Steve Lomas's challenge on Bergkamp wasn't the worst the Dutchman suffered in 1997–98. But something seemed to snap. Bergkamp swung an arm backwards and hit Lomas in the face. Referee Mike Reed reached for the red card. 'I knew then I'd have a busy evening,' smiled Manninger. He did.

Anelka's strike from the edge of the box gave Arsenal the lead in the forty-second minute. Hartson levelled, collecting John Moncur's pass, then curling a shot past Manninger.

Extra time couldn't separate the teams; it was down to penalties again. Hartson felt West Ham should have won in 120 minutes. 'After Arsenal had lost probably their best player, we felt we had a really good chance, even when Anelka put them in front,' he said. 'I have to admit, we created very little against a very solid defence – that's Arsenal. Then it went to penalties. Penalties are a lottery. You could lose to the Dog and Duck on penalties.'

It was 2–2 on spot kicks and Remi Garde had just missed, when Manninger dived right and tipped Berkovic's shot against a post. Patrick Vieira netted for Arsenal. Lomas replied for the Hammers. Then the pressure was on Adams to score for the Gunners. 'If I'd thought about it long enough, I might not have taken it,' he recalled. 'But we were running out of penalty takers. So my plan was to get it over with as quickly as possible – which thankfully I did.'

Samassi Abou had to score to keep West Ham in contention. He ran up, and shot wide of Manninger against the post. Arsenal were through after another nail-biter. 'I'm very pleased we have gone through – but

Christopher Wreh scores the only goal of the semi-final against Wolves.

these finishes are not good for my nerves,' smiled Wenger, probably the coolest man at Upton Park.

The semi-final was a re-run of nineteen years before. Then, Pat Rice was Arsenal's right-back and captain. The Gunners, without the injured Liam Brady, had seen off Wolves 2–0 before going on to beat Manchester United at Wembley. This time, Bergkamp was suspended because of his dismissal at West Ham. 'Of course we'll miss Dennis. But we weren't a one-man team in 1979 and we're not a one-man team in 1998,' said Rice. 'It's up to everyone else to make up for Dennis's absence. So many of our players have come through so many pressure games – Tony Adams, Lee Dixon, Nigel Winterburn, for instance – that they know just what to expect. We'll be treating the semi-final like a normal away trip; another game at Villa, if you like.'

The match was settled after twelve minutes. Wolves' keeper Hans Segers scuffed a kick out. Vieira controlled the ball and hurtled forward. He released his pass to Chris Wreh at just the right moment. As Segers advanced, Wreh buried his shot to the keeper's right: 1–0 to the Arsenal. For Wreh, cousin of George Weah and a refugee from Liberia's civil war, it was the highlight of his career. He celebrated with his trademark double somersault. 'I love to express the happiness I feel inside when the ball goes in the net,' said Wreh.

The only problem was that thousands of Arsenal fans who should have been inside Villa Park never saw the winner. A procession of Arsenal cars honked their horns in celebration of Wreh's goal – but they were still driving off the M6 at the time. The scenes were amazing as more than 4000 Gunners supporters were stuck on the motorway long after kick-off. The cause of the hold-up was never apparent, though the blocking off of one exit off the M6 at junction 6 may have had something to do with it. The local police had a helicopter flying over the motorway so they must have known the chaos going on below. Maybe television was a crucial influence. Had Sky Sports – with flexible schedules – been screening the game live, a thirty-minute delay would have been possible. But it was ITV's match and they were locked into immovable schedules, unless there was extra time. At pitch side, David Dein was imploring FA officials to put back the kick-off; but to no avail. He later sent a stinging letter to the FA on behalf of the Arsenal fans.

Wolves manager Mark McGhee knew the reason for Arsenal's success: Vieira. 'He was amazing,' said the Wolves boss. 'He's the fittest player I've seen in a long time. At his best, he reminds me of Graeme Souness: harassing opponents, setting the tempo, dominating games with his energy. The tempo he keeps is unbelievable. He breaks things down. He chases people into making mistakes and he has a tremendous tackle on him. And he doesn't even seem to break sweat.'

Vieira, named Man of the Match, commented: 'Now I've had a full season in English football, I feel so much fitter and stronger than I did at this stage last season. I'm sure there's more to come from me, and the rest of the players.'

Wenger still had his mind fixed on the Championship, always his priority. But he knew enough about the traditions of the Cup to tell the media: 'Cup competitions are not important in some countries. England is something else. I won the French Cup with Monaco and the J-Cup in Japan with Grampus Eight. But when you think of 'the Cup', you think of England, and the final at Wembley.'

Wreh's goal – coming so soon after a vital winner at Bolton – had vindicated the manager's faith too. 'I'm pleased with the way he's adapted to the English game,' said Wenger. 'It hasn't been easy for him. Two months ago, he was virtually unknown outside Highbury. Since then, he has grown and grown in confidence.'

So to Wembley, and Newcastle. The Geordie club had beaten Arsenal – in fortuitous circumstances each time – in the 1932 and 1952 finals. 'I believe we're capable of beating any team in the country and I want to tell my grandchildren about how we beat Arsenal and lifted the FA Cup in 1998,' said Newcastle skipper Rob Lee. Instead, it would be Lee's former Hornchurch neighbour, Adams, who lifted the Cup. It wasn't Lee's fault. He was one of Newcastle's few positives on a negative afternoon.

Arsenal were missing star names. Bergkamp, out with a hamstring injury since the league game against Derby, failed a fitness test the morning before the match. Wenger also decided not to risk Wright, who'd started just two league matches since the Port Vale replay. But Arsenal won the final with pace. Newcastle defended with a back four so far upfield that any ball over the top invited Overmars and Anelka to outrun them. Newcastle fans wondered why Kenny Dalglish hadn't used a sweeper.

Warren Barton was supposed to be double-teaming on Overmars with Alessandro Pistone. Overmars ran and ran for the right position. After twenty-three minutes, it came. Barton had taken himself out of range. Petit chipped over the Newcastle defence, and Overmars burst clear to nutmeg Shay Given. Anelka had already headed over from Parlour's cross. Wreh and Parlour missed more chances. But no one could criticise Parlour. He was Man of the Match by a street. Running inside and outside Newcastle's defenders, creating chances with crosses, or bursting inside himself, he cut a magnificent figure. 'He's come on so much,' said Rice. 'He can do it all now: run, tackle, pass and shoot.'

'Arsène Wenger has given me a chance,' said Parlour. 'He encouraged me to do things with the ball, and that gave me confidence. He told me to take on defenders and try and dictate the game. He's backed me even when I haven't done things quite right. I couldn't ask for more. It's great man management and encouragement.' Anelka says the same.

'People forget that Anelka's only a teenager,' said Wenger. 'He has had to grow stronger and learn a lot – and that's what he's done. It was hard for him when he came into the side. He had no experience at Premier level. He was physically below what was required. So he lacked confidence. But as he started scoring goals – and acquiring the necessary experience for the Championship – he developed game by game. He's strong now. In the Cup final, he held off challenges he wouldn't have resisted earlier in the season. And his natural talent and pace are shining through.'

Never more so than for the Gunners' second goal. The Geordies were threatening Arsenal's one-goal lead. Nikos Dabizas had hit the bar. Alan Shearer struck a post. Arsenal needed a killer blow. Anelka supplied it, shredding Newcastle's offside trap, outpacing the cover, then scoring with a blistering cross shot. 'He can go on to become a world-class striker,' beamed Wenger.

The Cup – and the Double – were on their way to Highbury. Amid the celebrations, how many even remembered Port Vale in January?

Pat Rice congratulates Arsène Wenger at the final whistle at Wembley.

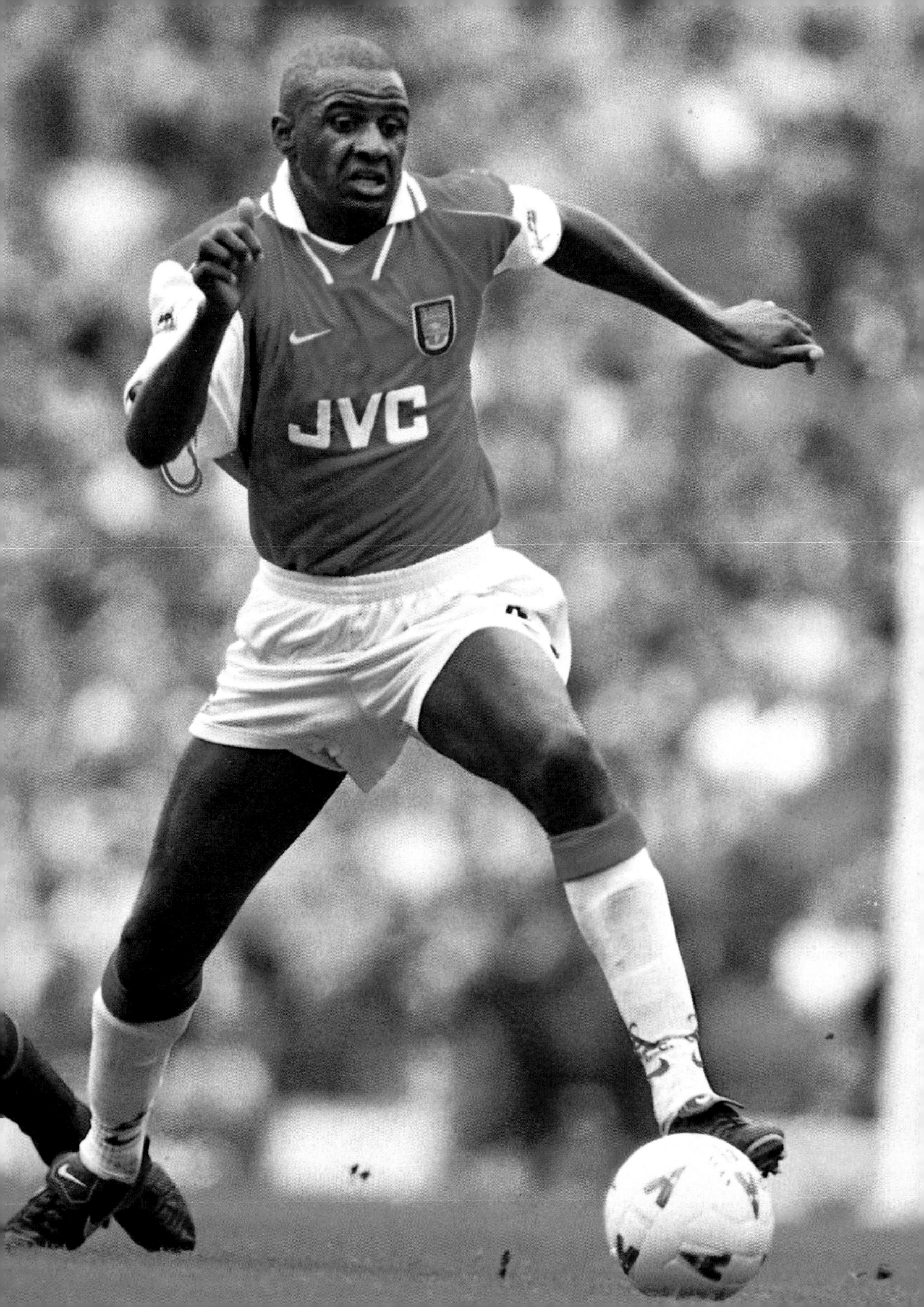
JVC

MIDFIELD WARRIORS

Don Howe, who knows about coaching Double teams, calls them 'the powerhouses behind Arsenal's success'. Yet Ray Parlour, Patrick Vieira and Manu Petit seemed an unlikely combination last summer. Vieira had already established himself as a player of huge potential, but Parlour wasn't even sure of a regular place; while Petit was an unknown quantity to most Arsenal fans: a centre back who'd played a season-and-a-half in midfield for French champions Monaco. By the time Arsenal won the Double, Vieira and Petit were fêted as the Premiership's top central midfield pair, and Parlour had leapt into England contention.

'We're all aware of the strength of the defence; and in attack, players like Bergkamp, Overmars and Anelka can make a goal out of nothing,' said Howe. 'But for me, the main reason for the team's ascendancy has been the midfield trio: Ray, Patrick and Manu. They've been magnificent in defence and attack. They're all such powerhouses. They have finesse too, and in the last few months of the season, no opposition midfield seemed to be able to live with them.'

Arsène Wenger's tactical switch – allocating Vieira and Petit more protective duties without reining in their attacking instincts – was crucial to the Gunners' success. As Wenger said: 'Their co-ordination not only launches our attacks, it also makes life difficult for players trying to get at our defence.'

Wenger introduced Petit to the Highbury fans, promising: 'He is a great worker, with excellent vision and a good left foot.' It took a while for Petit to settle in. He also admitted that he felt his natural position was centre half, though few would have realised that by the end of the season. 'I had to go through a process of adaptation, which was only natural because so many aspects of my life had changed,' he said. 'In the first few games, I was surprised too because I kept seeing the ball fly over my head, and I thought that wasn't good for spectators or players.'

Patrick Vieira, a powerhouse in central midfield.

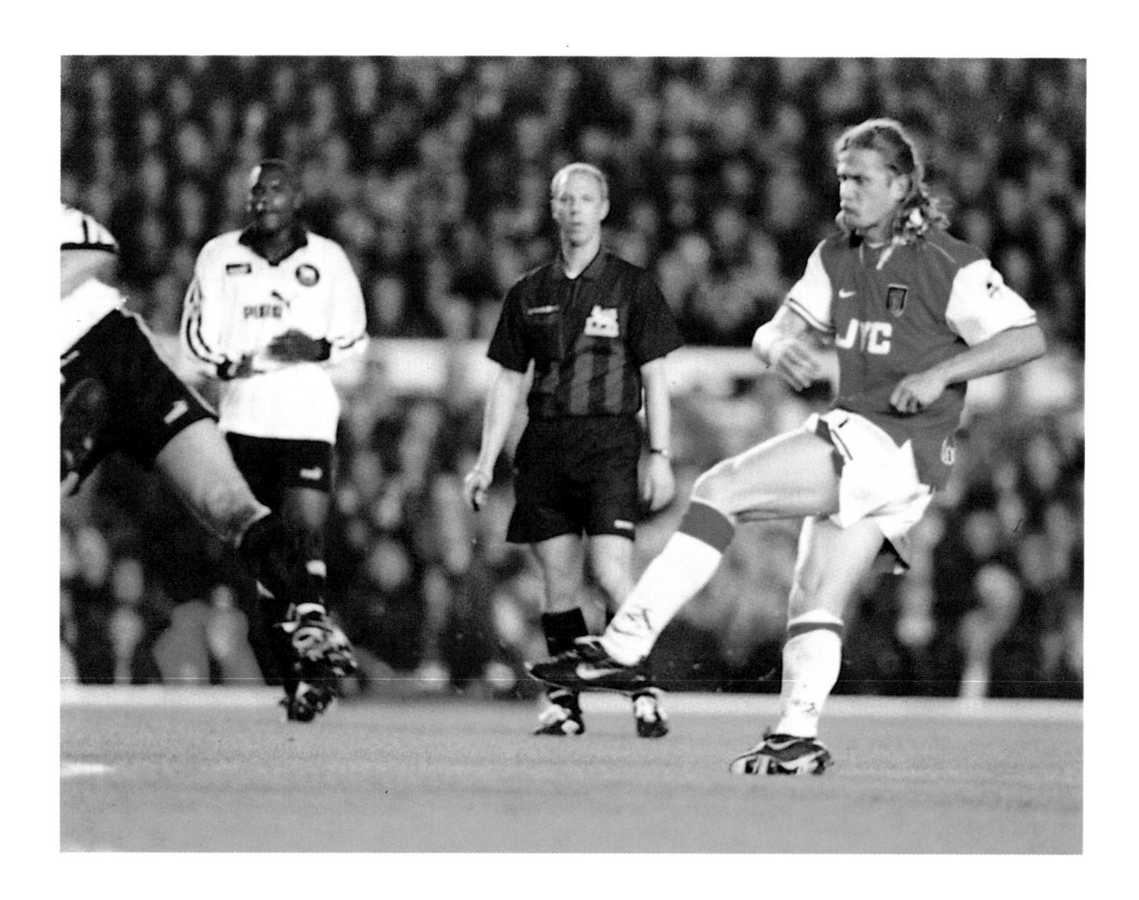

Manu Petit cracks the winner against Derby.

Petit's suspension after he was red-carded against Aston Villa also held up his progress, and at Christmas, the fans were still undecided. By February though, Petit was starting to enjoy himself and the supporters began to see the difference. 'I feel as if I've got used to English football,' he said. 'I have learned about fighting and commitment. I believe I will achieve a higher level of performance now that I have adjusted.'

He was immense when Arsenal won at Old Trafford, combining physical presence with shrewd distribution. The way he broke into the box demonstrated his growing confidence. 'It was only a matter of time,' smiled Wenger, after Petit had scored his first goal in the 5–0 win over Wimbledon. Eleven days later, he struck an even more vital shot: the goal that beat Derby and set up the Championship carnival against Everton. 'The goal against Wimbledon gave him composure to shoot, knowing his technique was sound,' said Wenger. 'And he could have scored again with two free kicks.' Petit's countryman, Spurs winger David Ginola, summed up Petit's new-found stature. 'He's one of the best central midfielders in the country, maybe in Europe,' said Ginola. 'He is happy and intelligent on the ball and he has all the physical strength that the English game demands.'

Ginola was equally effusive about Vieira. 'He's quick, he's strong, and he's so intelligent with his use of the ball. As a Frenchman, it makes me proud to see him and the other French players in the Arsenal squad do so well.' 'I think Patrick is the best holding midfield player around,' said Petit. 'I'm not sure what Milan were thinking when they sold him, but they must regret it now. And he's so young. He'll get better and have many successful years ahead of him.'

As Wenger pointed out, Vieira is two-footed, with a wide passing range, a stinging shot – as he showed against Newcastle at Highbury – and a powerful tackle. He has energy to burn too. 'It's great to think he's still only twenty-two,' said Tony Adams.

For Vieira, the experience he gained in 1996–97 was vital to his role in Arsenal's Double triumph. 'Having had one season in the Premiership already, I felt much stronger and fitter than I did the previous year,' he said.

Vieira is a big admirer of the Ajax, Milan and Holland great, Frank Rijkaard. He tries to play in the same style. 'He's the player I've learned most from,' said Vieira. 'Like him, I try to win challenges, then keep possession and keep the ball moving, ideally with a nice through-pass for our attackers.'

Vieira's one flaw was his disciplinary record. Dismissals at Coventry and in the Coca-Cola Cup semi-final second leg at Chelsea, plus incidents in both FA Cup ties against West Ham, landed him in trouble with the authorities at Lancaster Gate. Wenger made his feelings clear. He wanted Vieira on the pitch, not serving bans. In the final few weeks of 1997–98 it looked like the message was getting through. Vieira collected only one yellow card in his last eleven appearances. 'I spoke to the manager and the other players and I thought a lot about what had been happening,' said Vieira. 'I tried to learn.'

Like most others at Highbury, Vieira was surprised that Parlour didn't make England's final party for France '98. After the Cup final – when Parlour won the Man of the Match award – Vieira commented, 'I find it very hard to understand why Ray is not even in England's final thirty. He had a fantastic game today and he has been outstanding all season.'

Pat Rice, who once coached him in Arsenal's youth team, analysed Parlour's contribution: 'His energy and his ability on the ball have been a revelation.' Parlour attributes the blooming of his talent to his own change in attitude – and to the encouragement he received from Wenger. Recalled Parlour: 'When we came back for pre-season training, I didn't know where I stood with so many new players added to the squad. But I'd done a lot of thinking over the summer and tried to sort my life out.'

The influence of a settled relationship and two young children (the youngest, Frankie, born during the season) helped Parlour set things in perspective. So did the experiences of Paul Merson and Tony Adams. 'While I'd not encountered the

Ray Parlour hits the third goal against Bolton at Highbury.

problems they had, it made me stop and think,' he said. 'I thought of two very talented players who were close to losing it all and that forced me to get myself in order. I did some silly things during my younger days which earned me a reputation for being a bit wild. I'd like to think I've changed my behaviour, and I'm reaping the rewards on the pitch.'

Parlour has always had a 'good engine'. Now he added technical quality and valuable goals, like his two at Blackburn on Easter Monday. 'He has practised very hard and he has grown more confident with every success,' said Wenger. 'He has been magnificent, and his form at Wembley was everything I could have asked for.'

Parlour had been in and around the side since 1992, but it was Wenger who offered him a regular run. 'He gave me a chance and that lifted my confidence,' said Parlour. 'He didn't get on my back if I made a mistake. I've worked hard and steadily improved. A lot of that is down to man-management.'

Behind the formidable trio was former England captain David Platt. When he joined Arsenal from Sampdoria in the summer of 1995, he said he was coming home to win something in England. He'd finished a Championship runner-up with Aston Villa in 1990. He'd won a UEFA Cup winner's medal with Juventus and an Italian Cup winner's medal for Sampdoria. 'It was a wrench to leave Genoa. I had two fantastic years there. But I wanted to win Championships and cups here.'

Platt started only eleven league games and one in the FA Cup, although he seemed to come on as a substitute in virtually every match. He replaced the injured Petit in the

Championship finale against Everton, then came on for Chris Wreh in the second half at Wembley. 'It gives any manager confidence to have a player of his experience to send on to the field,' said Wenger.

Maybe the way Platt's season worked out wasn't quite how he'd intended to win those Championships and cups . . . though Gunners fans will long recall his winning header against Manchester United at Highbury. But he turned down opportunities to move – to become a player/manager or manager – to stay with Arsenal. 'I didn't feel that the offers I received were right at the time,' he said. But Platt never complained, never played the prima donna, the 1990 World Cup hero, or Serie A star. He was the 'good pro', in the proper sense of that much-abused phrase. 'The squad system has been very important for Arsenal, particularly over the last three months of the season,' he said. 'It really was a spirit of "one for all and all for one".'

Just like the three guys Don Howe was talking about.

David Platt, a vital member of the squad.

Travel

ARSÈNE

The banner that hung over the front of the west stand said it all: Arsène Knows. So did the cheers from the thousands outside Islington town hall on 17 May 1998, when Manager of the Year Arsène Wenger stepped out to hold Arsenal's trophies aloft for the crowd.

Herbert Chapman made the Gunners great. Wenger has made them popular. In the long term, he may be remembered even more for that achievement than the Championship and cups he brought to Highbury. It was a new feeling for Arsenal fans. Even dyed-in-the-wool Spurs supporters – like the *Evening Standard*'s Matthew Norman and Richard Littlejohn of the *Sun* – congratulated Wenger's team for the football they played. Millions seemed to be willing Arsenal to overtake Manchester United. Most of the neutrals wanted the Gunners to beat Newcastle at Wembley too. Imagine that three or four years ago!

Arsène Wenger issues instructions.

As Alan Smith, top scorer in the 1989 and 1991 Championship years pointed out, those sides contained some gifted midfielders and attackers – Smudge himself, Paul Merson, David Rocastle, Paul Davis, Mickey Thomas, Brian Marwood and Anders Limpar. George Graham still believes those teams never received the praise they deserved. He's probably right. But there was a difference about Highbury in those days – a feeling of Arsenal against the world, heightened by the 1990–91 points deduction after the brawl at Old Trafford. Graham's teams drew strength from that spirit. Wenger, arriving from France via Japan, carried none of that baggage.

He spoke good English already, which gave him a head start over some foreign coaches. It may be his third language, but he expresses himself with a lucidity that puts many British-born managers to shame. The press like him because he always fills their notebooks. Wenger is a very private person, but he'll talk for ages about football. It says a lot about Wenger's character that – despite the totally unfounded allegations about his private life that greeted him when he arrived in England – he's always ready to chat with the media.

He doesn't duck issues either – well, only when an Arsenal player has done something he shouldn't. 'I didn't see it,' he'll smile, knowing the media don't believe him; and knowing that they know he knows. Wenger will make his point in private, as he did with Patrick Vieira after the West Ham cup tie at Highbury. But he will never, ever criticise one of his players in public. As Wenger says: 'It's not only what you say that matters. Sometimes what you don't say can be just as important.' The players realise it, and respect him for it.

Behind the charm, there's huge substance and fierce determination. Earlier in the season, a northern manager wondered to a group of journalists if Wenger lacked the passion to succeed in England. That was to misunderstand Wenger. He cares, desperately – witness his reaction after the home defeats by Liverpool and Blackburn – but effing and blinding from the dug-out is not his style. Maybe his time with Grampus Eight in Japan had an influence. Glenn Hoddle, who played under Wenger at Monaco, remembered a coach who could lay into players verbally. But football management in Japan is different. Shouting is seen as losing face. Aggressive displays are considered bad manners. 'That's part of Japanese culture, to respect each other,' recalled Wenger. 'It was the same with the Grampus fans. They went crazy when the team won. But they were never negative or aggressive when we lost. I was glad about that. When I look back on my time in Japan, I think I learned a lot.'

It was Wenger's passionate intensity that set the tone for Arsenal's run-in to the title. Graham was ferociously single-minded. So is Wenger. Only the next match mattered. Two years ago, Alex Ferguson's psychological games rattled Kevin Keegan in full view of the nation. There was no chance of that with Wenger. The Arsenal manager smiled at every comment from Old Trafford – and kept concentrating on the next match. 'There was a huge amount of pressure on the team, but the manager was very good at keeping it off the players; very good at relaxing us,' said Martin Keown. 'He seemed so unruffled and we all drew strength from his coolness. He made us very, very focused.'

Wenger also kept his nerve – or what's called 'bottle' in north London. He showed it early in his tenure, when he addressed an impromptu press conference on the stadium steps, to nail the slurs on his good name. He showed it again over Christmas and new year, when Arsenal's prospects looked distinctly rocky. He steadfastly believed results would improve once Arsenal's injured and suspended players returned. He also listened to his squad. Wenger didn't just *call* that decisive team meeting after the defeat by Blackburn, he *acted* on the results. Revised, more guarded roles for Vieira and Manu Petit were crucial to the Gunners' solidity and success.

Wenger may be a good listener, but he can be stubborn when he believes he's right.

While so many managers – including his protégé, Glenn Hoddle – have experimented with three at the back, Wenger has stuck to 4–4–2. He loves to play with width, to stretch opponents with pace. It's no accident that Arsenal have probably their fastest attack in living memory. As Smith said: 'This must be the quickest strike force I've seen at Highbury. Marc Overmars, Dennis Bergkamp, Nicolas Anelka and Ian Wright are all so quick off the mark.'

Unlike Ferguson – and Ruud Gullit and Gianluca Vialli too – Wenger knows his strongest team and sticks to it. He lets the opposition worry about Arsenal. As Nigel Winterburn said: 'We don't change our line-up to deal with who we're playing. We go out to play *our* game.' Wenger likes players who can fight a bit too. Not kick or hurt opponents, but players like Vieira and Petit who'll stick a foot in to win a vital tackle. The way he talked about Alan Shearer after the incident with Neil Lennon was revealing. 'Maybe if Shearer didn't have aggression he would not be such an effective striker.'

Wenger keeps faith with players he believes in. He stuck by Overmars, even when he was substituting the Dutch winger regularly. He backed the young talent of Nicolas Anelka, even when Highbury fans were calling for a big-money signing. He supported the potential of Chris Wreh, even when the Liberian striker looked way off the pace before Christmas. His reward has been goals from these players that made vital contributions to Arsenal's success. As the banner said, Arsène knows.

Arsène Wenger with his Manager of the Month award for March.

Wenger's attention to diet and physiological preparation is famous. Stretching exercises – plyometrics – have become part of the Gunners' routine, followed by rigorously planned exercises to the tick of the manager's stopwatch. Wenger employed a full-time masseur. On the food side, chips and red meat were soon forbidden. In came grilled meat and fish, rice and green vegetables – like the ubiquitous broccoli – instead. Wenger sees himself as an educator about health as well as a coach. He's as far removed as it's possible to be from the Premier manager who once described the culture of English football as 'train, play, then get plenty of lager down your throat'. The players accepted Wenger's ideas because they could see the benefits. 'He's certainly extended my career,' said Steve Bould. 'I wish I'd had this sort of preparation when I was younger,' says Lee Dixon: 'Players listen because they realise that if they look after themselves they can prolong their careers at the top.'

Wenger benefited hugely from the Arsenal board's 1995 change of policy, when the club swept away a rigid wage structure and signalled its intentions by signing Dennis Bergkamp and David Platt. Wenger himself gained immediate street cred with the fans after recommending that Arsenal rescue Vieira from the bench at AC Milan. Last summer, the directors backed Wenger all the way as he re-shaped the Arsenal squad. Bruce Rioch – who gave the club a long list of targets, though none were signed – might have been surprised at that transfer activity.

Wenger's priority was pace and penetration on the flanks, which is why Overmars arrived from Ajax. The Monaco trio – Petit, the versatile Gilles Grimandi and Wreh – added depth to the squad. Winger Luis Boa Morte and midfielder Alberto Mendez were players for the future. The ex-Graz goalkeeper Alex Manninger already looks another prominent example of Wenger's judgement. Wenger only signed one English player: defender Matthew Upson from Luton, whom Tony Adams already views as his long-term successor. Wenger regrets he couldn't sign more Englishmen. 'But I had to strengthen the squad quickly, and the sort of players I wanted weren't available here,' he reflected.

For a man who never grew up at Arsenal, Wenger has shown a huge respect for the club's traditions. 'I love the spirit of the players, the determination to succeed and the passion of the supporters,' he says. He has stuck with the famous back four – the 'soul' of the club – while grafting on the extras he planned to add when he arrived: 'Technical qualities; to improve our movement and speed of attack. To work on the way we move without the ball. To bring creativity.'

He's also had some help. The board supported him throughout the difficult months. Pat Rice has played a key role. They may seem like chalk and cheese, the economics graduate from Alsace and the Belfast boy who grew up in Islington. But they both love the Arsenal. It's no coincidence that Wenger, who prefers to avoid confrontation, leaves many of the day-to-day minutiae of organisation and discipline to Rice. Pat Rice, 1971 Double winner, then the Arsenal skipper, is steeped in the Highbury way of doing things. His value has been as adviser and confidant. 'Pat knows Arsenal inside out. He's honest and he's loyal, and he knows all about the other English clubs. His knowledge has been very important to me,' said Wenger.

It's also typical of Wenger that he preferred to harness Rice's vast local knowledge rather than bring in his own number two, even if he did add his old colleague Boro Primorac to the coaching staff. The ebulliently efficient Gary Lewin – physio to England as well as Arsenal – completed a formidable back-up team.

It's a long way from Wenger, the amateur who played for Strasbourg, to Wenger, the successful manager at Highbury. Maybe, though, the seeds of Wenger's management success had already been sown more than twenty years ago, when he learned so much from his own mentor, the former Strasbourg coach Max Hild. As Strasbourg's old retainers say, Wenger may not have been good enough to play consistently at top level, but his personality had a powerful influence on the rest of the squad, especially the youngsters breaking into the first team.

George Weah, his protégé at Monaco, regards Wenger as the biggest and most beneficial influence on his career. At Highbury, Adams talks about the support Wenger afforded after the Blackburn defeat, when the Gunners captain wondered if he could maintain his own standards. Wenger arranged the trip to the south of France, from which Adams returned a vibrant figure. Then there's Ray Parlour. Parlour himself has made huge lifestyle changes which have helped him rise to the brink of the England squad. Undoubtedly, 1997–98 was his finest season. He also acknowledges Wenger's backing: 'It's nice to be encouraged, rather than hollered at.'

But what Wenger has done most of all is to liberate Arsenal from fear. Yes, the defence has to be sound. Yes, Vieira and Petit have to be strong in the centre of midfield. But Bergkamp, Overmars, Parlour and Anelka all have licence to play. So do the people behind them, when it's 'on'.

Wenger was delighted when Petit scored against Wimbledon – and continued with the vital goal against Derby. And Adams' goal, the fourth in the Championship finale against Everton, gave him special pleasure. 'That was a symbol of the way we want to play,' he said. Bould made it with a delicate chip. Adams tucked it away like a forward. 'He's told us that we should attack whenever we can, because other players will fill the gaps behind us,' said Bould. 'He's not ruled by fear. He encourages us to go out and play,' said Adams.

Meanwhile, wins over Newcastle, Wimbledon and Everton on the title run-in, plus the Bergkamp-inspired demolition of Blackburn at Ewood Park earned the Gunners applause throughout the land. As chairman Peter Hill-Wood, a fan for nearly fifty years, put it: 'I love watching this team. We've scored so many wonderful goals. We play attractive football, we pass well, and I think Dennis Bergkamp is the best player in the league.' The 1989 and 1991 teams could play a bit as well. Maybe they were damned with faint praise. But, as philosophers say, 'There's no such thing as reality, only perceptions of it.' In those perceptions, Hill-Wood expresses the popular opinion.

Matthew Norman wrote of Wenger in the *Evening Standard*: 'The halo can't be far away.' Arsenal fans, being demanding souls, will settle for the Champions League.

The Gunners will enter the Champions League with a fund of goodwill, because the new Arsenal are admired as well as respected. That is the measure of Wenger's achievement.

POSTSCRIPT

'How do you follow that?' the media asked Arsène Wenger after the Gunners had beaten Newcastle at Wembley.

'Our first task is to win the Championship again,' he replied.

Arsenal's history shows it's easier said than done. No Arsenal manager since George Allison continued Herbert Chapman's master plan in the 1930s has presided over back-to-back titles. Not even the great Tom Whittaker, or George Graham. Graham came so close to building his own dynasty at Highbury. But in 1990 and 1992, the years after his Championship successes, the Gunners were never realistic challengers.

As Wenger said: 'It will be important to start well, especially with so many of our players coming back from the World Cup. They need to be right, physically and mentally. We know the other teams will all be looking for us, because we're the champions. Mind you, they look for us anyway, because we're Arsenal!'

And the Champions League?

Wenger, ever the shrewd psychologist, has already lifted the pressure off the players by asserting that it's almost impossible for a Premiership team to win the Champions League because of the congestion caused by the English fixture list. 'The English programme will not allow it,' said Wenger. 'Competing in the Champions League is not a level playing field for English clubs.' Wenger repeated that view after watching Real Madrid pip Juventus 1–0 in the Champions League final. Real's win meant that Arsenal, as seventh seeds, will go into a group including another big-name seeded team too. 'There was nothing I saw which made me reconsider my assessment of English clubs' chances in the Champions League,' he said. 'There's too much stacked against it. As I said, the Championship has to be my priority, then the Champions League. There are many

Above Arsenal champions; Arsène Wenger says retaining the title will be top priority.

Below Real Madrid celebrate winning the European Champions Cup after beating Juventus in the final in Amsterdam.

CARLING
CHAMPIONS
CARLING
F.A. PREMIERSHIP
JVC
CARLING CHAMPIONS

REAL MADRID

Chairman Peter Hill-Wood.

things we would have to improve even to give us an opportunity of winning it. For instance, we have to learn how to keep possession better. But our players possess a tremendous attitude to do well.'

David Platt is sure Arsenal will gain from the experience. 'Ninety minutes against the likes of Juventus or Real Madrid leaves you mentally exhausted, but that experience is priceless,' he said. 'Look at what the Manchester United players have gleaned from playing at the highest level. A lot of the United team may be relatively young – but not in footballing terms.'

But then, at Christmas, it seemed almost impossible that Arsenal could win the Double. The test for the Gunners is to build on that success. The 1971 Double side never won another trophy. That summer, Bertie Mee's right-hand man, coach Don Howe, left to become manager at his old club, West Bromwich. It was a crucial departure. The following season, Arsenal finished fifth in the league, lost the FA Cup final to Leeds and went out of the European Cup – somewhat unluckily – to Ajax, the greatest club side of the time: Johan Cruyff, Johan Neeskens, Piet Keizer, Ruud Krol and all.

At Christmas, Bertie Mee had tried to strengthen the squad by paying a club record £220,000 to Everton for England midfielder Alan Ball. Ball replaced Jon Sammels, who'd moved to Leicester that summer. Too little, too late? As Pat Rice remembered: 'When Don left, it was a great blow, because he'd been so influential. Some players were unsettled. We could still compete right at the top, but we didn't seem to click again, like we did in the Double season.'

In 1972–73, Mee's side finished runners-up to Liverpool, and lost the FA Cup semi-final to second division Sunderland. With hindsight, that was the time the team started breaking up. Things will be different, twenty-seven years later. Firstly, Wenger is going nowhere. Neither is Rice. Vice-chairman David Dein pinpointed Wenger as a potential Arsenal manager years ago. As Dein said after the Wembley victory, 'Arsène is now the hottest managerial property in Europe – but we're confident we can keep him at Highbury!' Secondly, chairman Peter Hill-Wood has promised the manager substantial funds, to supplement the squad and compete in the Champions League.

Targets? One of the most interesting questions posed to Wenger after the Wembley triumph was, 'Will you be looking for a centre forward who can head the ball, to give you more options in attack?'

Wenger smiled. 'You know the players you would like. Sometimes you can get them, sometimes not – but I would like to keep our squad together – and sign more players.' By the time you read this, you'll know the outcome.

Liam Brady, head of youth development.

'He's been very shrewd in the transfer market,' says Hill-Wood. 'He doesn't just judge on ability. He also looks at players' characters, and only wants people who can fit in with the spirit of the club.'

Arsenal's squad will be bigger and stronger than it was in 1972, when long-term injuries to Bob McNab and Eddie Kelly reduced Mee's options to the bare bones, and the Gunners ended up playing more matches than they'll face next season. George Graham, on the losing side against Ajax in 1972, comments: 'Arsenal have a strong squad. They've shown they can cope with injuries and suspensions and they came on very fast towards the end of the season. Patrick Vieira and Manu Petit have the ability – plus the physical and mental strength – to be key players in the Champions League. Arsène has handled everything very astutely and he knows just what's required in Europe.'

Alan Smith marked his European Cup debut with four goals in a 6–1 slaughter of Austria Wien in 1991. He believes the Gunners are well-equipped to compete with Europe's best. 'Arsenal can soak up pressure and score goals on the break,' he says. 'Look at their pace in attack, with Marc Overmars, Dennis Bergkamp – and Nicolas Anelka coming into his own.' But Graham and Smith share one worry: Bergkamp's fear of flying. Bergkamp's absence in Salonika was vital when the Gunners went out of the UEFA Cup to PAOK. 'If Arsenal are drawn in Moscow, well, it's a long train journey,' says Graham. Says Smith: 'It's a problem for

Arsenal's vice-chairman, David Dein, celebrates with Arsène Wenger.

Arsenal, if they have to replace Bergkamp, though Anelka has come on in leaps and bounds since Christmas.'

The other query is the old chestnut: how long can the Gunners' legendary defence carry on? That will be one of Wenger's toughest decisions, deciding when to reshape the back line. As Nigel Winterburn says, 'Every season, we read that this is our last, but we just keep on playing.'

But Tony Adams believes Wenger has found his long-term successor in teenage centre-back Matthew Upson. 'I'm already trying to show him the ropes in my position,' said Adams. 'He has a lovely left foot and he looks a great prospect. I think it was Don Howe who tipped us off about him. Recommendations don't come much better than that. He reminds me of myself at that age. He's a fast and willing learner. He's a perfectionist who's never satisfied with his form, and that can only be good for Arsenal.'

Upson, signed from Luton last May, is one of the Gunners' young Englishmen on the rise. Wenger hopes many more will develop through Arsenal's revitalised youth programme, headed by Highbury great Liam Brady. 'I wanted to sign more young English players last summer, but they weren't available, so I had to go to Europe,' said Wenger. 'It's part of Arsenal's tradition that every successful side contains a nucleus of players who've come through the youth team. In a few years' time, I hope that will be so again.'

For the first time in more than twenty years, the Gunners ran two youth teams in 1997–98. The Premier Youth League side won the league's southern conference, then edged Spurs 2–1 on aggregate in the inaugural play-off finals. They also won the Southern Junior Floodlit Cup, beating QPR 2–0 in the two-leg final. In 1998–99, however, the Gunners will leave the South East Counties League after more than forty years and concentrate on Premier Youth League football for Under-19s and Under-17s. 'I'm sorry about that, because I began my career in the South East Counties, and the league made a big contribution to the development of so many players,' says Brady. 'But long term it's better for our youngsters' progress if they compete against the best young players from the other top clubs in the country.'

Howe, who returned last summer, has made a huge impact as head youth coach. 'He's a terrific influence. He has so much experience and knowledge,' says Brady. 'He and the other coaches, Don Givens and Neil Banfield, have set very high standards and the boys have responded to the quality of the coaching.'

Islington-born midfielder Paolo Vernazza has played twice for the first team. Jamie Day earned a squad number in February. Brian McGovern was already a pro. Tommy Black, David Livermore, Greg Lincoln, Allan McLeod, Omer Riza and Julian Gray have earned pro contracts for 1998–99. 'Potentially they're an exciting group,' says Brady. 'Now they must aim to break into the first team squad over the next two seasons.'

The club expect to have a purpose-built centre for promising schoolboys up and running within the next eighteen months, preceded by a new training ground close to Arsenal's old Hertfordshire base at London Colney. The Gunners received planning permission from Hertsmere Council in February, and the complex is due to be finished next summer. Says managing director Ken Friar: 'The new training ground will provide eight pitches and a building containing state-of-the-art facilities for senior and youth players.' That's vital to Wenger – and Brady. 'I'm very excited by the plans,' says Brady. 'We aim to have the best training facilities in Britain.'

Meanwhile, after the breakdown of the proposed move to Wembley, negotiations continue with Islington Council about developing Highbury. When Arsenal are successful, the 38,300 capacity is clearly too small. The Gunners could have sold 50,000 tickets for most of their closing games. As Friar says: 'Costs, particularly players' wages, are rising but the club can't fit more fans into the stadium to meet them.'

But the Gunners approach 1998–99 upbeat. Says 1971 Double skipper Frank McLintock: 'Arsène's team are as well organised as we were. Tony Adams is a very good leader on the pitch. They have the same resilience and spirit that we had. Their Double has been a terrific achievement and I hope they go on from there.'

Charlie George, Arsenal's 1971 Wembley hero, believes Wenger's squad can. 'They have strength in depth and they have pace and variety,' he says. Adds Rice: 'Arsène wants to strengthen the squad and if his buys are like the players he's brought in so far, then we can be very optimistic.'

Hill-Wood agrees. 'I enjoy watching this team more than I've ever enjoyed watching an Arsenal team. The expectations next season will be enormous – but I'm looking forward to another exciting year. It should be fun!'

MATCH-BY-MATCH RESULTS 1997-98

DATE	OPPONENTS	VENUE	SCORE	GOALSCORERS	CROWD
FA CARLING PREMIERSHIP					
Aug 9	Leeds United	A	1-1	Wright	37,993
Aug 11	Coventry City	H	2-0	Wright 2	37,324
Aug 23	Southampton	A	3-1	Bergkamp 2, Overmars	15,246
Aug 27	Leicester City	A	3-3	Bergkamp 3	21,089
Aug 30	Tottenham Hotspur	H	0-0		38,102
Sept 13	Bolton Wanderers	H	4-1	Wright 3, Parlour	38,138
Sept 21	Chelsea	A	3-2	Bergkamp 2, Winterburn	33,012
Sept 24	West Ham United	H	4-0	Overmars 2, Wright(p), Bergkamp	38,012
Sept 27	Everton	A	2-2	Wright, Overmars	35,457
Oct 4	Barnsley	H	5-0	Bergkamp 2, Parlour, Wright, Platt	38,049
Oct 18	Crystal Palace	A	0-0		26,180
Oct 26	Aston Villa	H	0-0		38,061
Nov1	Derby County	A	0-3		30,004
Nov 9	Manchester United	H	3-2	Anelka, Vieira, Platt	38,205
Nov 22	Sheffield Wednesday	A	0-2		34,373
Nov 30	Liverpool	H	0-1		38,094
Dec 6	Newcastle United	A	1-0	Wright	36,751
Dec 13	Blackburn Rovers	H	1-3	Overmars	38,147
Dec 26	Leicester City	H	2-1	Platt, own goal	38,023
Dec 28	Tottenham Hotspur	A	1-1	Parlour	29,610
Jan 10	Leeds United	H	2-1	Overmars 2	38,018
Jan 17	Coventry City	A	2-2	Bergkamp, Anelka	22,864
Jan 31	Southampton	H	3-0	Bergkamp, Adams, Anelka	38,056
Feb 8	Chelsea	H	2-0	Hughes 2	38,083
Feb 21	Crystal Palace	H	1-0	Grimandi	38,094
Mar 2	West Ham United	A	0-0		25,717
Mar 11	Wimbledon	A	1-0	Wreh	22,291
Mar 14	Manchester United	A	1-0	Overmars	55,174
Mar 28	Sheffield Wednesday	H	1-0	Bergkamp	38,087
Mar 31	Bolton Wanderers	A	1-0	Wreh	25,000
April 11	Newcastle United	H	3-1	Anelka 2, Vieira	38,102
April 13	Blackburn Rovers	A	4-1	Bergkamp, Parlour 2, Anelka	28,212
April 18	Wimbledon	H	5-0	Adams, Overmars, Bergkamp, Petit, Wreh	38,024
April 25	Barnsley	A	2-0	Bergkamp, Overmars	18,691
April 29	Derby County	H	1-0	Petit	38,121
May 3	Everton	H	4-0	own goal, Overmars 2, Adams	38,269
May 6	Liverpool	A	0-4		44,417
May 10	Aston Villa	A	0-1		39,372
ARSENAL'S FINAL RECORD					
Pld: 38	W: 23	D: 9	L: 6	F: 68 A: 33	Pts: 78
UEFA CUP					
Sept 16	R 1, 1st leg PAOK Salonika	A	0-1		33,117
Sept 30	R 1, 2nd leg PAOK Salonika	H	1-1	Bergkamp	37,982
COCA-COLA CUP					
Oct 14	R 3 Birmingham City	H	4-1	(a.e.t) Boa Morte 2, Platt(p), Mendez	27,097
Nov 18	R 4 Coventry City	H	1-0	(a.e.t) Bergkamp	30,199
Jan 6	QF West Ham United	A	2-1	Wright, Overmars	24,770
Jan 28	S/F, 1st leg Chelsea	H	2-1	Overmars, Hughes	38,114
Feb 18	S/F, 2nd leg Chelsea	A	1-3	Bergkamp(p)	34,330
FA CUP					
Jan 3	R 3 Port Vale	H	0-0		37,471
Jan 24	R 3 Replay Port Vale	A	1-1	Bergkamp Won on penalties 4-3 after extra time	14,964
Jan 24	R 4 Middlesbrough	A	2-1	Overmars, Parlour	28,264
Feb 15	R 5 Crystal Palace	H	0-0		37,164
Feb 25	R 5 Replay Crystal Palace	A	2-1	Anelka, Bergkamp	15,674
Mar 8	R 6 West Ham United	H	1-1	Bergkamp(p)	38,077
Mar 17	R 6 Replay West Ham United	A	1-1	Anelka Won on penalties 4-3 after extra time	25,859
April 5	S/F Wolverhampton Wanderers	Villa Park	1-0	Wreh	39,372
May 16	FINAL Newcastle United	Wembley	2-0	Overmars, Anelka	79,193

PLAYERS' PREMIERSHIP APPEARANCES AND GOALS

Nigel Winterburn 35+1(1) Ray Parlour 34(5) Manu Petit 32(2) Marc Overmars 32(12) Patrick Vieira 31+2(2) David Seaman 31 Dennis Bergkamp 28(16) Lee Dixon 26+2 Tony Adams 26(3) Ian Wright 22+2(10,1p) Steve Bould 21+3 Martin Keown 18 Nicolas Anelka 16+10(6) Gilles Grimandi 16+6(1) David Platt 11+20(3) Stephen Hughes 7+10(2) Christopher Wreh 7+9(3) Alex Manninger 7 Remi Garde 6+4 Matthew Upson 5 Luis Boa Morte 4+11 Scott Marshall 1+2 Alberto Mendez 1+2 Paolo Vernazza 1 Isaiah Rankin 0+1 Gavin McGowan 0+1 own goal (2)

+ = substitute appearances; goals scored in brackets